THE DIVINE GARBO

'THE DIVINE GARBO is a must both for its revealing text and most complete collection of Garbo pictures ever assembled.' – DAILY MAIL

'The exclusive interview with Garbo, extravagantly illustrated . . . An essential addition to all Garbo "collections".' – FILMS & FILMING

'My Book of the Month must be "THE DIVINE GARBO". A superb Christmas gift for almost anybody.' – SCREEN INTERNATIONAL

'This sumptuous, beautifully produced volume will surely come as close as any ever will to solving the "Garbo Enigma" . . . crammed with fascinating detail and fresh insight. It's all stunningly printed and embellished with a large number of really unique photographs. These illustrations are a treasure house in themselves.' – FILM REVIEW

'Much of the mystery that is Garbo is unveiled in a fascinating new book . . . called THE DIVINE GARBO. New insights into her relationships with men are also revealed for the first time in this beautifully presented book.' – PHOTOPLAY

THE DIVINE GARBO

Frederick Sands and Sven Broman

SIDGWICK & JACKSON
in association with New English Library, London

First published in Great Britain in 1979
by Sidgwick & Jackson Ltd, 1 Tavistock Chambers
Bloomsbury Way, London WC1A 2SG
Originally published in the United States of America in 1979
by Grosset & Dunlap, Inc.
First paperback edition published in 1981 by
Sidgwick & Jackson Limited
Copyright © 1979 by Frederick Sands
ISBN: 0-283-98752-9
Printed and bound in Great Britain by
Collins, Glasgow
for Sidgwick & Jackson Limited
1 Tavistock Chambers, Bloomsbury Way
London WC1A 2SG

Excerpts from *Here Lies the Heart* by Mercedes de Acosta
(Reynal & Co., 1960) by permission of
William Morrow & Company and André Deutsch Limited

Excerpts from *Garbo* by Norman Zierold published by
Stein and Day Publishers © 1969 by Norman Zierold

A selection from *Gayelord Hauser's Treasury of Secrets* by
Gayelord Hauser. Copyright © 1951, 1952, 1955, 1963 by
Gayelord Hauser. Reprinted with the permission of
Farrar, Straus & Giroux, Inc.

Excerpts from *Cecil Beaton: Memoirs of the 40's* by
Cecil Beaton, copyright © 1972 by Cecil Beaton, by
permission of McGraw-Hill Book Company

Excerpts from *The Strenuous Years: Diaries 1948-55* by
Cecil Beaton, copyright © 1973 by Cecil Beaton,
by permission of Rupert Crew Limited

CONTENTS

Acknowledgments

Our thanks go to all who have submitted patiently to our questioning about Greta Garbo — but most of all to Garbo herself for affording us the exceptional opportunity of getting to know her at first hand.

Many people have helped us with personal reminiscences of and anecdotes about the celebrated star from her earliest days, giving generously of their time and advice. Without their help we would still be in a jungle of a seemingly impossible task — to write a book about the *true* Garbo of today and all her yesterdays.

Our efforts were concentrated on seeking out hitherto untapped sources of information in interviews with people who knew or know Garbo and would talk about her for the first time, thereby avoiding as much as possible duplicating what has been written about Garbo before.

Without the constant encouragement of Robert Markel, our New York publisher's dynamic editor-in-chief, it is doubtful that we could have risen to the challenge. Also, for their special skills and good taste in putting the book together in its final form, our special gratitude goes to Nancy Brooks and Bette Alexander.

Frederick Sands and Sven Broman

Introduction

Like any writer concerned with celebrities, I had always wanted to meet the divine — and elusive — Garbo, and I came to regard an interview with her as the ultimate goal of my craft, not least because no journalist in the past decade or more had been able to pull it off. Although all predictable odds were certainly against me, I never completely gave up hope that one day I might be the lucky one.

I was. When I met Garbo in the summer of 1977, my story made headlines around the world, some of them reminiscent of M-G-M's slogan to promote *Anna Christie*, her first sound film: "GARBO TALKS!" Sweden's biggest magazine, *Året Runt*, called it "the interview all journalists have been dreaming about."

The meeting itself, when it came, was a chance encounter — but one for which I had carefully laid the groundwork. I had begun serious efforts to obtain an introduction to Garbo in New York the previous year. These had been unsuccessful, but they produced valuable information about Garbo's annual summer pilgrimages to Klosters in the Swiss Alps. I spoke with friends who have a holiday home in Klosters and who had frequently seen Garbo strolling through the village behind her dark glasses. They told me about her habit of long walks and described her daily routine as they had observed it. I learned the location of the small apartment she keeps in Klosters, and the usual date of her arrival and length of her stay. Most important, I learned that her visits to Switzerland are not solely to escape the summer heat of New York, but to spend time with an old friend, Salka Viertel. After a distinguished career in Europe and Hollywood as actress, teacher, and scriptwriter — she had worked on the screenplays for five major Garbo films — Salka Viertel had retired to Klosters, where each summer in the years before her death in 1978 she welcomed the

7

visits of her younger friend and former colleague. This knowledge was the first light — for I too knew Salka, and was confident that I could count on her help when the time came. It seemed clear that the best ground for a meeting with Garbo would be Switzerland, not New York.

But by now it was fall, and Garbo had already made that year's visit and returned to New York. A year would pass before the next opportunity. I spent those months bringing myself up to date as far as possible on Garbo's past and present life. I felt I had a slim but real chance of meeting her in favorable, informal circumstances, and my hopes for a successful story were based on the possibility of talking with her as long and as fully as she might allow. Still, a private meeting such as I hoped for would have to be documented. There would have to be proof, the proof only photographs can give convincingly. It would be utterly foolish to think that Garbo would agree to pose for a picture with me, even in the best of circumstances. And yet I needed those pictures.

Eckhard Nitsche is a photographer of the old school. In pursuit of a subject no effort is too much, no hours too long, no discomfort too great. When he accepted the assignment to go to Klosters he had no idea what was in store for him. His briefing simply instructed him to bring warm clothing — and cameras with telescopic lenses, which were to be packed in his luggage so as not to identify his profession. I met Nitsche at the train station when he arrived in Klosters in August 1977 and took him to his hotel, where I explained his mission: to take candid — and clandestine — photographs of Garbo with me. The opportunity for such photographs might come at any time, at any place. I would give Nitsche advance notice if possible, but as Garbo's next move is always unpredictable, he would actually have to keep me under surveillance at all times and hope. Above all, there was never to be any sign of recognition between us. His endurance and mobility would be put to the test.

8

Nitsche rose to the occasion. He immediately reconnoitered the village and familiarized himself with the location and layout of Garbo's apartment house, which has two entrances and can be approached from different directions. By the end of his first day in Klosters he had taken rooms at three strategically located hotels, and had hired a car and driver to be at his disposal every day from morning till night. His enterprise and ingenuity knew no limits.

As in previous years, Garbo had arrived in Klosters in the middle of July; I had come two weeks later, planning to give Garbo time to settle down before making any approach. Shortly after my arrival, I heard that my aged friend Salka Viertel had become a homebound invalid. It was natural, then, that I would visit her often during my stay, and each morning around eleven o'clock I walked up the creaky wooden stairs to her apartment. There, propped up on a settee, a black woolen shawl over her legs for warmth, she would receive me.

Salka had trouble hearing, and she spoke with difficulty. I soon noticed that she would quickly grow tired, so I kept my visits short despite her constant promptings to stay longer. "Why are you always in a hurry to go?" she would ask. One morning, as I was about to take my leave, she said in her frail, barely audible voice, "Come back for tea this afternoon. You'll meet someone interesting."

On several of my visits Salka had mentioned that Garbo was in Klosters and was dropping in to see her every day. It took all the self-control I could muster not to show overmuch interest, except to say that I would be delighted at the chance of meeting her. So Salka's invitation to tea, phrased as it was, had to be it. I alerted Nitsche to be ready.

"Whatever you do, don't let her see you," I warned him, "or she might take flight and never come back."

At four o'clock I returned to Salka's apartment. Her companion-nurse had laid the table for tea. A short while later Garbo arrived. For a moment she remained standing in the doorway, hesitant at the sight of a stranger. Then, at her friend's beckoning, she came into the room. Introductions were simple and brief. They seemed to satisfy Garbo, and she strode to the table and poured tea for us. "Milk and sugar?" she asked me without looking up, and I thought I saw her blushing slightly. And moments later we were seated side by side on a wooden bench at the table, munching homemade cake and chatting comfortably.

Garbo was dressed in a beige turtleneck sweater and checked brown trousers. She wore no make-up except for a dash of lipstick, and her fingernails were short and unpolished. Her salt-and-pepper hair was held together at the back by an elastic band, her forehead covered by a fringe of bangs.

She did most of the talking that afternoon, beginning by describing her walk that morning, and complaining about the weather (it had begun to rain) and how cold she was in her apartment: "Last year I became very ill here and thought I was going to die. They never put on the heating, no matter how cold it gets." Conversation continued casually; Garbo knew only that I was a friend of Salka's, and had no idea I was a journalist. I had hoped to remain "anonymous" for a while, as we relaxed and got to know each other. But Garbo lit a long black cigarette and turned to reach for an ashtray on the windowsill behind her. The ashtray rested on a book. And the author's name on the jacket was mine.

The book was *Charlie and Oona Chaplin: The Story of a Marriage*. I had brought it for Salka that morning because she had known Chaplin in Hollywood.

Garbo's attention was caught. She picked up the book, her eyes resting on my name. She turned it over, and as if to resolve any doubt, the back of the jacket carried a photograph of me with Chaplin at his desk. There was a moment of silence, during which Garbo reached for her dark glasses, which she had taken off while we had our tea. Then she turned to me and said accusingly, "So you're a writer. I don't like writers. They're dangerous people."

I cursed myself for having brought the book, fearing that all was over before it had begun. But miraculously Garbo was not put off. She was now leafing through the book, stopping every now and then to ask a question or comment on a picture. "This is a lovely one," she said, pointing at a photograph of Charlie and his beautiful Oona and their eight children, lined up in pipe-organ fashion against the background of their imposing Swiss mansion. She wanted to know how long I had known the celebrated actor, and how we had met. The critical moment had passed. For the next two hours Garbo spoke freely about herself, her life, her retirement. My "dangerous" vocation was forgotten — or forgiven.

The Garbo I met that afternoon had retained her slim, youthful figure. The beauty of her famous eyes and unforgettable features still shone. If time had not stood still — even for Garbo — since the heady days of her triumphs, her looks did not betray her years. Nor was her manner that of a woman in her seventies, then or on later occasions when we met. We spoke in English, and she talked in a melodious, sometimes throaty voice with an intriguing mixture of American and European accents. Now and then she would throw in a word of German, French, or Italian to emphasize a point when she could not find a suitably expressive English word. When she talks, her finely shaped hands gesture in rhythm with her words. When she listens, it almost seems you can read her thoughts — her attention is complete, and her eyes never leave your face.

The afternoon flew, and it was time to leave Salka. Garbo and I left the apartment together, and found ourselves in pouring rain. I had walked to Salka's before the rain had started, and my car was at my hotel, some distance away.

Garbo's apartment was just across the road from Salka's, and she had come prepared with an umbrella. Now Garbo

11

was holding her umbrella over both our heads, and we began to walk quickly toward her house.

"I'll lend you another umbrella to get you back," she said on the way. I blessed the rain, uncomfortable as it was. If I borrowed Garbo's umbrella I would have to return it, and that would mean seeing her again. Standing in her doorway, I asked if we could meet the following day. Garbo thought for a moment and then said, "Let's wait and see what the weather is like." She knew where I was staying and added, "I'll call you at ten." I kissed her lightly on both cheeks, and thanked her for a wonderful afternoon. Then, sheltered by Greta Garbo's spare umbrella, I trudged back to my hotel overjoyed.

There was a message from Nitsche waiting for me. I returned his call and asked him to come to my hotel room. When he arrived he reported that there had been no safe place for him to shelter from the rain and still keep us within camera range either at Salka's apartment or at Garbo's. Nevertheless, he had waited for hours in the rain before finally giving up only when darkness fell — using flash was out of the question. He poured himself a stiff Scotch to warm up and ease his disappointment. His spirits lifted when I told him of the possibility of another meeting with Garbo the next day and her promise to call me in the morning. Meanwhile, all we could do was wait and keep our fingers crossed.

The next day was cold and drizzly, and low black clouds hung over the Alps. I hoped the weather was not a bad omen, but a cheerful-sounding Garbo telephoned on the dot of ten. Thoughtfully she asked whether I had a mackintosh and some warm clothes, and when I reassured her she suggested that if I would care to go for a walk with her despite the weather I should meet her in an hour's time. "Don't come to my house. Meet me outside Salka's," she instructed me.

I obeyed, but this time I went by car, parking so that I would see her leaving her house. When she came out she looked around her, apparently to assure she was not being followed,

12

and walked over to my car slipping into the seat beside me. She carried a small black plastic bag: this, she explained, contained waterproof trousers which she could put on if it began to rain heavily. She suggested we drive to Davos, ten miles away, and walk around the lake — a two-and-a-half-mile hike. She was dressed sensibly for such an outing, wearing a wool-lined black anorak, tweed trousers, and stout boots. She seemed completely relaxed and in a happy mood. "To hell with the weather," she said, "let's enjoy ourselves."

As we started off she told me that she did not like to drive fast — which proved helpful to Nitsche's driver, who followed us at a discreet distance on the short but winding journey.

Conversation flowed easily as we drove. She had taken off her dark glasses and looked directly at me all the time, never at the road ahead. I could feel her eyes searching out mine, which I found disconcerting at times — especially when approaching a hairpin bend. As I drove with both hands on the wheel, at one point she even linked arms with me.

From the start, less than twenty-four hours before, I had felt free to call her Greta. Now, all of a sudden, she reprimanded me. "Don't call me Greta. I hate that name," she said.

Taken aback, I asked, "What should I call you, then? Miss Garbo, perhaps? It sounds so out of tune."

My face must have betrayed my feelings at this moment, and Garbo came to my rescue at once. "Call me G.G.," she said. "So much nicer, don't you think?" Then she smiled as only Garbo can and added, "I think I'll call you Sandy. Do you like that?"

The morning of my departure from Klosters the sky was blue, the sun shone bright. I found myself wanting very much to see Garbo again. I had her telephone number and could not resist the temptation to use it. Garbo agreed readily to meet in an hour for breakfast.

As I got ready to pick her up, I remembered that her birthday on September 18 was not far off, and I wanted to make her a small gift. But what does one give a woman who can buy anything she wants for herself? Then I recalled Garbo's smoking habits. It had mildly irritated me every time she attempted to light one of her favorite black cigarettes with a cheap throwaway lighter that seldom worked. I would go out and buy her the best one I could find in the short time I had before we were to meet. I was in luck. I found a small gold lighter of a well-known make and had it beautifully wrapped in a gift package.

When I gave it to her over breakfast, wishing her a happy birthday, she took the package with almost childish delight and tried to guess what it might contain. After a few playful moments, during which she hugged me, she finally removed the decorative wrapping and opened the box.

"Oh no!" she exclaimed when she saw the contents. "I can't accept this. Please take it back."

Seeing my disappointment, Garbo explained, "I have a whole drawerful of expensive lighters and never use them. You see, Sandy, I just hate having to look after nice things."

When I insisted that, nevertheless, I wanted her to have it and she must keep it, she relented — but not much. "Okay," she said, "then it will join all the others."

Soon afterward I drove her back to her apartment. She knew I had a long journey ahead of me, and said she wanted me to get to my destination before dark. "Call me when you arrive," she told me. And she dashed inside.

I had met Garbo, and I had a story. I also now had photographs: Nitsche's patience and skill had paid off, and he had been able to take pictures of Garbo and me at Lake Davos. Making notes in Garbo's presence was unthinkable, so I had spent long hours each night reliving the day's meeting and recording it in detail. As I wrote I tried to forget many of the things I had read or heard about her before we met: I found them intrusive, blurring and distorting my own impression of Garbo as I had come to know her.

As I worked I realized that the publication of my article about my meeting with the divine Garbo would only be the beginning of a search. She had talked to me with an unprecedented frankness that only increased my desire to portray and interpret this "mysterious lady" more fully than was possible within the restrictions of a magazine piece. I wanted to thread through the endless conjectures, assumptions, and outright falsehoods that have surrounded her life. The challenge of a book was irresistible.

I started at the beginning. I went to Stockholm, where Garbo lived until she left for America at the age of nineteen. There I renewed my acquaintance with Sven Broman, editor-in-chief of Året Runt. We had been colleagues since I began writing for magazines twenty years ago, and were good friends as well. I told him I wanted to continue my quest, and I was delighted when he agreed to work with me.

We began in the seemingly endless archives of Bonniers, the Swedish publishing organization that owns Året Runt. We spent a week simply sorting out files of rarely seen photographs, records, and ancient press cuttings. Aside from their intrinsic interest, these provided valuable clues to another kind of research. For we learned that there were people still living in Stockholm who had known Garbo — or Greta Gustafsson — as neighbor, schoolmate, employee, friend, fellow actor. Broman sought them out and talked with them, developing image by image, recollection by recollection, a new picture of Garbo.

For the period of Garbo's first years in Hollywood, Garbo speaks for herself in a series of letters she wrote between 1925 and 1928 to a friend in Sweden.

Broman concentrated on Garbo's life in Sweden; I followed her traces through later years, always hearing her voice, always remembering her as I knew her in Klosters.

Have we found the true Garbo? I do not know. A beauty, a talent, a presence like hers certainly defies analysis, possibly even description. But we worked in the light of the divine Garbo, and we hope this book will share her radiance.

Geneva, 1979

Chapter 1
CHILD

The Divine GARBO

Chapter 1
CHILD

At the turn of the century, Blekingegatan was one of the ugliest streets in the bleakest of working-class neighborhoods on the south side of Stockholm. Number 32, a five-story building demolished in 1973, looked out on permanently muddy vacant lots filled with broken glass. There, in a small apartment on the second floor — one room and kitchen — that at one time had to accommodate seven people, Greta Garbo lived with her family in near poverty until she left Sweden.

Greta Lovisa Gustafsson was born in the district Södra Maternity Hospital on September 18, 1905; her mother, Anna Lovisa, was thirty-three, a year younger than her husband, Karl Alfred. They had two other children, Sven, seven years old, and Alva Maria, two. An aunt, Maria Petersson, remembered it was an unseasonably cold day when the baby Greta was brought home from the hospital bundled up in a blanket held together with safety pins to protect her from the biting wind.

At the time of Greta's birth the Gustafssons were so poor that Karl's employer asked to adopt her. The man had no children of his own, and was eager to give the baby a good home. But Anna and Karl loved and wanted to keep their little girl. They considered the offer, but Anna finally declared: "If God gives you a child, he also gives you bread." And so Greta stayed at Blekingegatan.

Her parents had come to Stockholm from the agricultural south of Sweden seven years before, in 1898. It was an eventful year for them: they moved to Stockholm in April, they married in May, and Sven, their first child, was born ten weeks later, in July.

Karl Gustafsson had not wanted to leave the green pastures of his birthplace. His family had worked the land for generations, and he himself had spent most of his life on his father's farm where he had been born. But there was no work at home, and he went to Stockholm to find a job. Neither he nor Anna liked living at Blekingegatan 32, but it was all they could afford.

A silent and reserved man, Kalle, as his friends called him, was "different" from his Stockholm neighbors, but liked by them. He was gifted with a fine voice, and was at his happiest singing with the local choir. He was over six feet tall and handsome, and his photographs show a remarkable resemblance between him and his second daughter. Although he was only twenty-seven when he moved to the city, he suffered from severe kidney trouble. For relaxation he would take long walks alone.

Unskilled in any trade, the only job Karl could find in Stockholm was as a streetsweeper in his own district, which was inhabited mostly by laborers and small shopkeepers. The work often entailed lifting heavy barrels, and further weakened his health. The local custom was not to tip laborers with money, but to invite them in for a drink of local spirits or beer. For Karl this meant a fair amount of drinking, and often he would return home from a day's work visibly tipsy. To Anna's frequent reproaches he made the excuse that he needed the drinks to endure the monotony of a job he hated. When Karl could not find a better job, Anna called him a weakling.

As time went on, she treated him with growing contempt.

Anna was a robust, energetic woman of peasant stock with no education but a rich store of fairy tales and songs to delight her children. Sven was her favorite and could do no wrong in his mother's eyes, although neighbors occasionally took a different view.

To the young Greta, her mother seemed severe, and she reserved her affection for her father. It was he who encouraged her even as a small child to sing and dance. She was only five years old when her aunt Maria found her one day deep in thought. "What are you thinking about?" she asked. "I am thinking," answered Greta, "of being grown up and becoming a great actress."

Greta was especially fond of her father's brother, Uncle David, who was a taxi driver. He was the most affluent of the Gustafssons, owning a fine house and a car. Uncle David never came to visit without a bag of sweets for the girls, and gave them money and generally indulged them. To Uncle David the young Greta confided, "I'm going to become a prima donna or a princess and when I'm rich I'll give all I can to poor children."

But in later years her memory did not keep pace with her fame. David Gustafsson recalled the time when Greta returned to Sweden on her first visit home from Hollywood. "She invited us for Christmas Eve, insisting that we bring our little girl. Not until late in the evening did she discover that she had forgotten to buy her a single Christmas present."

A neighbor at Number 32 was Mrs. Karin Gustafsson, no relation to Greta's family. Mrs. Gustafsson was a widow and worked as a dressmaker. She also had the only telephone in the house, of which Greta became the most frequent user.

"I made all the dresses for Greta and her mother and sister for 1.50 kronor [thirty cents] a dress. That was in 1910 and it was very cheap, but Greta's mother always wanted to haggle," Mrs. Gustafsson told Sven Broman in Stockholm before she died at the age of eighty-four.

Greta, who was known as Kata in the neighborhood, was a real little cadger in those days. On paydays when the men came home from work she would stand in the street smiling at them with an outstretched hand, and getting the odd ten öre [a dime] here and there, which she would use to pay for her telephone calls.

As a child she daydreamed a lot and I remember her saying often, "When I grow up I shall live in lots of big rooms."

One day she came and asked me to make her a pair of gym shorts. She was seventeen and had just been accepted for the theater school. She wanted me to make them in silk, but I told her it would be too expensive.

On her first visit to Stockholm after moving to Hollywood she brought a Christmas present for me. It was the last time I saw her. Later I wrote to thank her for it. I addressed the letter only "Greta Garbo, USA," believing that she was so famous it would find her. But the letter was returned to me marked "unknown."

Shortly before she was seven, Greta entered nearby Catherina School, where she remained until she was fourteen. Her school records show her to have been a "fair" student, but lazy — her mind anywhere except on her lessons. Pupils were given grades A, a, ab, ba, B, in descending order from "excellent." On Greta's card the ab's predominate, with some general improvement in her last year. Like all pupils who were not actual terrorists in the classroom, she was consistently marked A for "Conduct" and "Diligence." But she often did not do her homework, and the only subject that interested her at all was history. She was absent only sixteen days in all — despite running away three times.

At twelve, tired of school, she and two other girls successfully traveled eight miles before they were recognized by an old lady in a shop, who called the police and had them sent back home.

The following year she ran off once more, this time to Skåne in the south of Sweden, by hiding in the toilet of a train.

21

Eventually she was discovered by the conductor, who arranged for her return. This adventure earned Greta a bad report card: the entry reads, "Unauthorized absence of one day."

Her third escapade occurred in 1919, in the summer of her last year at school. The children of poor families were sent to a holiday camp at Björkö, a small island in Lake Mälaren. Greta, who in her youth suffered often from sinus trouble, felt ill and disappeared after being told to help in the kitchen. The next day she turned up unexpectedly at home.

She returned to a family in trouble. Karl was now seriously ill and unable to work. Anna, Sven, and Alva all had to find jobs, and so Greta left school to care for her father at home and accompany him on visits to the district clinic. The months of sickness dragged on, and winter came. It was a hard and terrible winter, for the influenza epidemic had now reached Sweden, and thousands died. Still her father lived. Trying to fight poverty, illness, and the bitter cold, the Salvation Army opened soup kitchens on the south side of Stockholm, where the Gustafssons lived. They also organized a show for the children of the neighborhood, in which the children themselves took part. Greta acted and sang in that entertainment — her first public appearance. Her performance was particularly noticed and praised by John Philipsson, treasurer of the Salvation Army, and he encouraged Greta's firm ambition "to become a great actress."

After a long and exhausting illness, Karl Gustafsson died on June 1, 1920, two weeks before fourteen-year-old Greta's confirmation. In the months before his death the resources of the Gustafsson household were further strained by the arrival of two newcomers: an unmarried neighborhood dairy maid called Elsa Haegerman and her illegitimate baby son, fathered by Greta's brother, Sven. Greta and her sister, Alva, had to sleep on one settee made into a bed at nights. Almost sixty years later the infant son, also called Sven, recalled: "My mother was ill for some months after my birth. I have been

22

told that Greta, who was then fourteen, took great care of me and liked to walk around with me in her arms."

In 1931 Garbo recalled her childhood in the Swedish magazine *Lektyr*:

It was eternally gray — those long winter's nights. My father would be sitting in a corner, scribbling figures on a newspaper. On the other side of the room my mother is repairing ragged old clothes, sighing. We children would be talking in very low voices, or just sitting silently. We are filled with anxiety, as if there is danger in the air. Such evenings are unforgettable for a sensitive girl.

Where we lived, all the houses and apartments looked alike, their ugliness matched by everything surrounding us. Even the grass gave up trying. Usually in May some greenery tried to grow amid the ugly wilderness. I watched it with tenderness and watered the few blades of grass each morning and night. But in spite of my care they languished and died. They died just as did the children in our forlorn neighborhood.

My sister! My little sister — I called her that, in spite of the fact that she was two years older than me. She had always been so fresh, so beautiful. And suddenly, she was ill. It started very slowly, and then . . . I had hoped that she would come to America and join me. She had been in movies in Sweden a little, and I am sure she had a future in the movies.

I was always sad as a child, for as long as I can think back. I hated crowds of people, and used to sit in a corner by myself, just thinking. I did not want to play very much. I did some skating or played with snowballs, but most of all I wanted to be alone with myself.

Although I was the youngest of the family, my parents always looked upon me as the oldest. I can hardly remember a time that I was ever very little, or as little as other children. I don't think anyone ever regarded me as a child. Young as I was, I always had my own opinions and my brother and sister let me make the decisions for us all. It has been said that I was prematurely grown up. I was tall as a child but did not grow any more after the age of twelve.

I cannot put a year to the time that my love for the theater first began. It seems as if I have always carried it inside me. Already when I was very small and could still hardly talk I had a certain mania to paint — not on paper, as most children do, but on my own face. With the aid of a small paintbox my father had given me I painted my lips and face, believing that this is what real actresses do. No one in my family could escape my paintbrush. Then I forced them, together with me, to perform big dramas, amid screams which would make any spectator doubt that I was in possession of my senses.

I never enjoyed playing with others, even with my sister and brother, but preferred to sit alone with my dolls and picture books, and I found my greatest pleasure in my childish dreams. Unfortunately I am still the same now — finding it difficult to adjust to other people.

As for my schooldays, I lived in a constant state of fear, disliking every moment of it and especially two subjects: geography and mathematics. I could never understand how anyone could be interested in faraway places, or in trying to solve such ridiculous problems as how many liters of water could pass through a tap of such and such width in one hour and fifteen minutes. I not only thought it was stupid to lose time with such questions, but to the astonishment of my teachers I even dared to say so out loud.

The only subject I really liked was history, which filled me with all kinds of dreams. I read my schoolbooks on history just as if they were novels and often let my fantasy wander. According to my fancies I might shorten the life of a cruel king and replace him by a romantic knight, or reawaken an unhappy queen centuries after her death.

When the history teacher asked me questions I started by giving the correct answers, but then would get carried away, spluttering forth with conjured-up visions of my own. When the teacher stopped me and told me to start again from the beginning, I could no longer remember what I had said before and turned red. My embarrassment was taken as proof of my ignorance and I would get the lowest marks.

I was fourteen years old when my father died, after a long, lingering illness. He was only forty-eight. From that time there was only sobbing and moaning to be heard in our home. My brother and sister would not even try to control their grief, and I often had to ask them to be quiet. To my mind a great tragedy should be borne silently. It seemed disgraceful to me to show it in front of all the neighbors by constant crying. My own sorrow was as deep as theirs, and for more than a year I cried myself to sleep every night. For a time after his death I was fighting an absurd urge to get up in the night and run to his grave to see that he had not been buried alive.

Our lives were always ruled by extreme poverty. Father's paltry wage was the only income we had to live on until his death. Now it became necessary for all of us to work. My brother and sister found jobs in various shops, earning a few kronor. I was still too young, and besides, my mother wanted me to stay at home with her. But we badly needed every penny, and soon afterward a friendly neighbor got me a job in one of the local barber shops. My work there consisted of lathering the men's faces, preparing them to be shaved by the barber. While he shaved one I would be putting soap on the next one's stubble.

I soon conquered my early shyness and a certain feeling of degradation, and was not at all unhappy anymore, knowing that I did a good job. I was never as proud as of my first week's wages.

One day a customer, watching her at work at Arthur Ekengren's barber shop on the Götgatan, spoke to the young lather-girl, and told her: "I can offer you a better job than this, if you want it." He was Kristian Bergström, the son of Paul U. Bergström, the founder and head of Sweden's largest department store, known as PUB.

When Greta reported for work at PUB on July 26, 1920, she was put in the millinery department to help unpack hats. She was paid what was to her a princely salary, 125 kronor a month (about twenty-five dollars).

Two weeks later, the store engaged Magdalena Hellberg as manager in charge of ready-made women's clothing, and transferred Greta to work in her department. She remained in the job for two years.

Miss Hellberg, now in her nineties, lives in a tastefully furnished apartment in downtown Stockholm. Bright-eyed and full of vitality, she was happy to reminisce to Sven Broman about her junior assistant of almost sixty years ago.

"I have countless memories of those two years in which Greta worked for our firm. There was something indescribably fascinating about this girl even then," Miss Hellberg said.

She was one of ten girls working in my department. She was conscientious about her duties, but she was always dreaming of movies and the theatre. She once told me, "It is all I ever think about."

She was very ambitious, quiet, and always took great care about her appearance. Even at her young age one could sense her self-restraint.

One day Mr. Bergström, the big boss of PUB, came asking me if I could suggest a suitable girl to model hats for our spring mail-order catalogue for 1921. Without hesitation I answered, "Miss Gustafsson should be perfect for that. She always looks clean and well-groomed and has such a good face."

Greta was thrilled when I told her about her new assignment. Knowing that it was I who had recommended her, she told me, "Aunt Hellberg can arrange anything for me. Oh, how happy I am!" It was probably the longest sentence I ever heard her say at any one time.

So it happened that five pictures of Greta Gustafsson appeared in fifty thousand copies of our spring catalogue, distributed all over Sweden. She was still only fifteen, but looked more like twenty.

That in spite of her shyness Greta wanted to be photo-model seemed proof of her burning desire to become an actress. At such times all her inhibitions seemed to vanish.

When the first photographs of her were shown around everybody was satisfied and considered them very good. They virtually provided the opening for Greta Gustafsson's movie career.

Stockholm's first film studio had been built in 1911, and others soon followed. In the next decade, particularly in the prosperity that came to Sweden after the end of World War I, the film industry grew and flourished. Its two giants were Victor Sjöström and Mauritz Stiller, and there were a host of lesser producers and directors as well. Greta continued to model for PUB and other Stockholm department stores, and it was not unlikely that a photogenic girl with modeling experience and a portfolio could find work as an extra or even in small roles. Greta haunted the studios and made friends who promised to look out for work for her. Her persistence was rewarded when she received an offer of a small part in *The Gay Cavalier*, a film being made by John Brunius for Skandia Films. She asked PUB for a week off from work without giving the true reason. Only her closest friends — and her sister Alva, who appeared as an extra — knew, and they were made to promise not to tell. Her bit part as a maidservant went unnoticed, and her name did not appear in the screen credits.

Miss Hellberg recalled that in 1922, to commemorate the store's fortieth anniversary, PUB produced a promotional film called *From Top to Toe*. "It was a story of a family with children whose home had been destroyed by fire. To replace their lost clothing, they go shopping at PUB. Greta played the part of one of the daughters, and was seen choosing dresses and hats.

"The film was a big undertaking for those days, and Greta radiated charm and showed talent. Away from the camera she was often worried and nervous, especially before the opening of fashion shows in which she was modeling. She used to say, 'There is no room for mistakes, and I get butterflies in my stomach.'"

Two other commercials followed, one in which Greta modeled clothes, the other a promotional film for bakery products in which she played a comic role, cramming herself with cream puffs and cookies. The films were directed by a commercial producer hired by PUB, Captain Ragnar Ring. Miss Hellberg remembers:

Captain Ring was also an actor. I could see that he was growing very fond of the young Greta, and I noticed that she, although still only sixteen or seventeen, responded to his attentions.

I cautioned her, saying, "Miss Gustafsson, you shouldn't be seeing a man so much older than yourself." Her short reply to my warning was, "Well, I'll always learn something."

To my surprise she discovered very soon that I had a close relative who was an actor at the Royal Dramatic Theatre. His name was Ivar Kåge. Greta was always putting questions to me about the theater which I could not answer, but I would promise to ask Ivar when I saw him. Soon I became an intermediary, transmitting questions from one and bringing back answers and advice from the other.

That Greta made such a great success in later years must be attributed chiefly to the fact that she was always ambitious, never gave up trying, and cautiously, but with determination, climbed every rung of the ladder until she reached her goal.

Greta had now appeared in four films, all within a year. Brief as her roles were, her mind was made up that this was to be her life from now on. Her chance came quickly. In 1922, a well-known Swedish comedy film director, Erik A. Petschler, needed a young girl for his new film, *Luffar-Petter (Peter the Tramp)*.

Walking along the Vasagatan, one of Stockholm's main shopping streets, Petschler's eyes fell on a girl looking into the window of a shoe store. "I was fascinated by her profile, and as I came closer, I saw her eyes and lips, which appealed to me greatly. I said to myself, 'There is something very special about this girl,' " Petschler recalled.

"As soon as she saw me looking at her she gave me the kind of glance which expressed more clearly than words, 'Go away and leave me alone!'

"She walked away hastily and left me pondering; I knew I had to have this girl for my film."

As it happened Petschler was in PUB the next day to choose various costume items, including hats, for the girls in his film. Greta recognized him instantly as the man whom she had seen looking at her outside the shoe store the previous day, Petschler remembered.

Suddenly the tables turned, and when she overheard why and for what reason I was looking at hats, she asked me boldly and outright if there was a chance for her to play a role in my film. She had acting experience, she said, adding that she had done film commercials for PUB.

No more was said that day, as I attended to the rest of my shopping, except that I gave her my number and asked her to call me.

The following morning she telephoned, told me her name was Greta Gustafsson, and said that she was in a call-box at PUB and therefore could not speak for long. We made an appointment to meet at my home that evening.

Petschler said that when Greta arrived he asked her if she could read him something aloud, and she answered very firmly: "Yes, I can."

"She read a school poem. Her voice did not impress me, but her appearance did, and so I gave her the part in my film. I told her that shooting would take about two weeks."

Greta had to ask PUB for permission to take a leave from work. This time she told her employers that she wanted the leave in order to be in a film. She did not expect to be paid while she would be away, but Mr. Bergström turned down her request.

Petschler himself went to see Bergström to plead Greta's cause, but Bergström remained adamant. It was against the principles of PUB to make such an exception for anyone, he insisted.

It was a hard decision for a girl in desperate need of a regular wage. Petschler had told her from the start that all he could pay her was ten kronor a day for fourteen days. Greta made her decision the next morning, and quit her job on July 7, 1922. She gave as the reason: "To enter the films."

Peter the Tramp opened at the Odeon Theatre in Stockholm on December 26, 1922. It was not very well reviewed, but a critic for the Swedish magazine *Swing* did single out the newcomer and wrote of Greta's performance: "Since Miss Gustafsson has so far had only the dubious pleasure of having to play a 'Bathing Beauty' for Mr. Erik A. Petschler in his fire department film, we have received no impression whatever of her capacity. It pleases us, though, to have the opportunity of noting a new name in Swedish films and we hope to have a chance to mention it again." With the article appeared a photograph, which was captioned: "Greta Gustafsson: May perhaps become a Swedish film star. Reason: Her Anglo-Saxon appearance."

Petschler's role was not over. Looking back on his discovery of Garbo, he recalled the next steps:

One day during a shooting break Greta came to me, telling me that she wanted to go on working in theater and movies, and asked how she should go about it.

I had no immediate plans for another film, but started to think of how I could help her. One of the two top directors in the business was a Finnish Jew of Russian origin who had come to Sweden and now dominated our film industry. His name was Mauritz Stiller, and I thought that perhaps he could use her. So I gave her his address.

Two days later Greta came to me, on the verge of tears. Stiller, she said, had no time to see her. I told her to keep her courage up and to call on him a second time. Greta did as told but Stiller must have been in a bad mood, for he almost shut the door on her, saying, "Go away, I have no time to see you."

Not wanting her to give in, I promised to call Stiller myself to try and arrange a meeting. It took her all her courage to go back for a third time.

Greta said of their meeting, "There he stood in the middle of the room, looking me up and down. Then he broke into a smile and said, 'So you are here again. You are a stubborn one. Now let me hear what you can do.' While he sat down I remained standing and started to recite a poem. After a while I thought that he had fallen asleep. Slowly raising his head, he asked for my telephone number and said he would call me."

Even if Greta was not encouraged by her interview, I knew that Stiller always kept his word. I told her that what she needed above all was more training, and that she should try to enter the Royal Dramatic Academy. I was able to help her with an introduction to Frans Enwall, a former director, who took an instant liking to her.

That was also the last time that I ever saw Greta Gustafsson-Garbo in person. I heard later that Stiller had been visiting the Academy and attended one of her performances. He was then casting for his film, *The Saga of Gösta Berling*, and invited her to come for screen tests to Råsunda, Stockholm's movie city. She passed them successfully and got her role in the film.

Some years later a big Hollywood star came on a visit to Stockholm. It was Greta Garbo. I did not meet her. People forget so easily . . .

Chapter 2
ACTRESS

The Divine GARBO

Chapter 2
ACTRESS

Greta followed Petschler's advice and appealed to Frans Enwall for help in getting a scholarship to the Academy of the Royal Dramatic Theatre in Stockholm.

"She was fully convinced of becoming a great star one day, and I believed her," Enwall recalled later. "She said she needed training and experience, but that she had no money to pay."

Her talent, although raw and unformed, was apparent to Enwall and he promised to coach her and recommend her for a scholarship, but he warned Greta not to raise her hopes too high: out of hundreds of applicants each year, only a handful were given scholarships. Enwall became sick a week later, just when Greta was to have her first session with him. His daughter Signe, herself an actress and teacher, took her on as a pupil.

Before Greta could apply to the Academy she would have to have a certificate from her school and a personal reference vouching for her good character and behavior. Most of the young aspirants had attended private schools and came from superior social backgrounds. Greta's "credentials" consisted of a certificate from Catherina School and a letter from Arthur

Ekengren stating that she had been a good lather-girl at his barber shop. One can imagine the eyebrow-raising among the members of the selection committee. Nevertheless, Greta was invited to audition.

The great day came at the end of August 1922. Filled with anxiety after a sleepless night of anticipation, Greta asked her brother Sven to take the day off from his job at a bakery to go with her.

At the Academy the candidates waited in a cheerless corridor as they were called in alphabetical order and led one at a time to a bare, dimly lit stage to perform their pieces before a solemn-faced panel of judges composed of actors, stage directors, writers, and Academy teachers.

"Looking at them from where I stood was the closest I ever came to fainting," Greta said later. "All I could think of at that moment was not wanting to go back to my job. I just had to succeed."

Signe Enwall had rehearsed her thoroughly for the occasion in three short excerpts from current stage plays. Greta went through them in a trance, and when the audition was over she could remember nothing about it.

She was still in a trance as she walked home to Blekinge-gatan, and when she got there she went straight to bed. The next three days were agonizing; she was incapable of doing anything while waiting to hear from the Academy. The answer came on the third day: she had been accepted. On receiving the news, the jubilant Greta told everyone, "I'm so happy, I think I'm going to die with joy!"

Three weeks later, on September 18, 1922, the new pupils reported for their first class. Among them was a girl named Mimi Pollak, who was soon to become one of Greta's best friends. In her autobiography, *Teaterlek*, published in Sweden, Mimi remembers that Greta wore a black dress and looked very pale on that first day at the Academy.

"There was a dead silence in the classroom until Mr. Ortengren, the teacher, asked us our names and ages," recalled Mimi. "Greta was so excited that instead of giving her age, she blurted out, 'It's my birthday!' Everyone, including the teacher, laughed and the ice was broken. Greta was seventeen."

When the roll call was over, the class was dismissed and the students told to get to know each other. Most of them went to a café next door, but Greta was afraid there would be too many people and wanted to go somewhere else. Mimi Pollak had a room nearby and suggested they go there. "We drank coffee and smoked until suddenly Greta started coughing terribly. When she recovered she said it had been the first cigarette she ever had," Mimi said.

Their friendship soon included a third student — Vera Schmiterlöw, who later became one of Sweden's leading actresses. Mimi remembers an occasion when the three girls were taken out to dinner by three young men.

We arranged to meet them at six o'clock outside the Stockholm Stadium. It was a bitterly cold evening and we were early, our feet freezing like lumps of ice while we waited. They arrived in three separate horse-drawn sleighs and took us to a smart restaurant on the outskirts of town. Greta rode with a man named Gösta, who seemed to be falling in love with her on the spot. [Gösta Kyhlberg, a young banker, was indeed smitten. He gave Garbo the green silk dress which she is wearing in the photograph. She liked both the picture, which she used as a publicity shot when she looked for modeling jobs, and the dress, which she later dyed black and kept for a long time as one of her favorites.]

At the restaurant we were shown into a private dining room. The men wore black tie and smelled of Eau de Portugal. We had goose served on silver plates and juicy pears for dessert. From across the table I saw Greta putting one of the pears into her handbag.

Next morning I arrived for classes at the last moment as Mr. Nils Personne, one of the teachers, was counting his flock. There was no sign of Greta. Noticing her absence, the teacher made a note in his book. The same moment the door burst open and a smiling Greta walked up to him, saying, "Look what I have brought you, Mr. Personne," and handed him a large, juicy pear. The teacher looked at it appreciatively and erased her absence from the record.

Among the drama schools of Europe, Stockholm's Royal Dramatic Academy was considered one of the most rigorous. A crowded daily schedule provided training in acting, dance and movement, voice and elocution, fencing, make-up, and theatre history. The teaching at the Academy was influenced by the Delsarte system, an approach to acting and movement based on the interrelationship of body, mind, and spirit — an early theory of "body language." Garbo was a hard-working student with an iron will to succeed. She kept a well-worn, oilcloth-bound notebook in which she meticulously noted the fundamentals of stage comportment, including how to hold a wineglass and how to dry your tears ("you do it with your ring finger"). Under the entry "How to Use My Head" appears the following:

Bending the head forward means submission to somebody else's knowledge, a confession of a truth; can also express tiredness, sympathy, and sincere understanding.

To bend the head backward means the contrary.

A head bent backward — proudness and haughtiness.
The forward-bent head — the mildly indulgent and patronizing.
The high-borne head — the calm, persistent.

Big ears indicate a good memory, small ears bad memory.

On the eyes and mouth, "of greatest importance in facial expression," she noted, "A person who wants to catch low sounds instinctively opens his mouth. This is characteristic of people who are hard of hearing." Lips, cheeks, nose, fingers, feet are treated in great detail, with lists of significant characteristics:

Fruity lips — sensuality.
A full lower lip — boastfulness.
A full upper lip — impudence.
Raised corners of the mouth — vanity; makes me more beautiful!

Other pages of the notebook contain notes on her scenes, and her lines in a minor role she performed in a production of the Royal Dramatic Theatre. One of these, including stage direction, was, "He doesn't like me anymore, and I don't want to live any longer. *(Fall down on chair and weep)*."

Discipline at the Academy bordered on the military, and the students lived frugally and with single-minded dedication.

"To relieve the monotony of our routine," remembered Mimi Pollak, "Greta and I invented two rabbits, which we called Gusten and Fingal. Each day we thought up some new stories about them. In our imagination they lived in Greta's home. One morning Greta came in looking very agitated. She said that one of the rabbits had grown very big, and the little one sucked blood from it because it also wanted to be big. The thought so revolted us that we put an end to our game."

There was only a small, narrow changing room which the girls from two classes had to share. "Greta was very smart," said Mimi. "She always came in last and so had the room almost to herself. We worked hard and with great enthusiasm, but sometimes we also cried with fatigue."

The Academy occupied two rooms tucked away high up in the tower of the Royal Dramatic Theatre. One was lined with mirrors and a ballet practice barre, the other was a classroom. Lessons began at nine o'clock with one hour of gymnastics. The students' evenings were taken up either attending performances at the Royal Dramatic Theatre or putting on workshop productions themselves. From time to time they were given minor parts in productions at the Theatre. Pupils on scholarships were paid fifty dollars a month to meet their living expenses during their first year, and another forty dollars a month if they passed a test to become "contract" pupils in the second year. (The Academy course was a two-year program, with a third year of training offered only to specially chosen "premier" pupils. From the class that entered in 1922, two premier pupils were designated: Greta Gustafsson and Alf Sjöberg, who was to become one of Sweden's most successful movie directors.)

Vera Schmiterlöw, one year older than Garbo, now lives in retirement in Stockholm. In an interview she recalled her schoolfriend to Sven Broman:

Shortage of money was Greta's chief worry at that time. Apart from the small grant she was paid as a scholarship pupil, we all got three kronor [sixty cents] a night as extras when we appeared in a play. But Greta was always philosophical about things.

I remember one occasion, a festival opening night, when all the ladies in the audience wore beautiful long dresses. We could see them from where we stood on the stage before the curtain went up. We both let out gasps of envy. Then Greta whispered to me, "Just remember that they have to go to the toilet like everybody else!"

We made extra money by modeling. Greta and I appeared in an advertisement for a new Lancia Lambda, for which we were each paid seventy-five kronor — fifteen dollars. That was big money for us.

I believe I was the only one whom Greta ever invited to her home, where I met her elder sister Alva and her mother. The three had something extraordinary in common: the longest and most beautiful eyelashes I ever saw. Alva was actually more beautiful than Greta, but not as gifted nor photogenic. She worshiped Greta and helped her with money whenever she could, as did her uncle David, a taxi driver.

In those days we were a small circle of three — Greta, Mimi Pollak, and I — and we spent most of our time together. Mauritz Stiller, our great film director then, had taken a special interest in us, watching our work. One day he invited us to his home, where he pronounced judgment on each: "Greta is the most beautiful of you three, Mimi the most intelligent, and Vera has the most aristocratic name."

Miss Schmiterlöw recalled that neither she nor Greta had a bathroom at home and so went each week to Sturebadet, the public baths in the center of town.

Greta had a beautiful body, but she was rather plump and Stiller had told her to slim. There was a shower-bath at the theater school and after everybody had left Greta stayed on, stretched out naked on the floor taking a hot shower. Day after day she would be lying on her stomach with the water spouting on her back as part of her slimming. She wanted to become figure-perfect in Stiller's eyes as quickly as possible. As her legs were also too fat she bandaged them tightly each night, especially around the ankles, to make them thin.

Miss Schmiterlöw said that after finishing lessons at four o'clock they were mostly too tired to go out in the evenings.

The beauty that she was, Greta was constantly invited out by young men for dinner. On the few occasions when she accepted, she would make it clear before that she had to be home early. There would be no playing about. Greta would never let herself go down in a horizontal position!

She was always shy and got scared when people stared at her. With friends in a small party she could be gay, though always reserved, afraid of saying the wrong thing. Most of us had had the opportunity of a better education than she, and coming from a government school had given her a complex.

Now and again Stiller would say to her, "Shut up! Don't talk!"

It was not really necessary, for Garbo seldom talked when there were others around.

She adored Stiller, but as far as I know there was never anything between them. Everyone knew that Stiller had a different kind of interest. He saw Greta as some beautiful raw material for him to shape into form. Greta accepted this wholeheartedly.

When Garbo visited Sweden in 1965, the three friends of more than forty years met for dinner in Mimi Pollak's home and sat up until the early hours of the morning reminiscing about their past. Vera Schmiterlöw remembers, "Greta repeated many times that our theatre school days was the happiest period in her life. She spoke with regret of the mistakes she made in later years. Not getting married, she said, was the greatest of them all. A close second was her failure in ever being able to conquer her shyness."

Greta was still in her first year at the Academy when Mauritz Stiller first inquired about her progress there. He had kept a watchful eye on the young Greta ever since Erik Petschler had sent her to him. Periodically he would ask the head of the Academy about her work, and he once came unannounced and incognito to one of her performances. He was starting work on a new film and had a role for her in mind. He asked Gustaf Molander, director of the Academy, to send Greta Gustafsson to his home for an interview. It was spring of 1923.

Mauritz Stiller was a successful film director who enjoyed playing the part of successful film director. He drove a bright yellow car and wore English-tailored suits and fur coats reaching to the ground. He was on terms of intimate friendship with the great, and was known to the maîtres d'hôtel of Europe's leading restaurants. Forty and over six feet tall, heavy featured, with gray hair and bushy brows, the flamboyant Stiller impressed everyone — especially young actresses.

Greta was predictably apprehensive when she made her way to Stiller's home for the appointed interview. She felt that her whole future depended on its outcome. But when she arrived at the house she was told that Stiller was out. Keeping people waiting, often for hours, was a deliberate shock treatment the director meted out to newcomers.

When Stiller finally arrived, two hours late, he found Greta taut and confused. Pretending to have forgotten the appointment, he made no attempt to put her at her ease while he looked her up and down. Then, after a few minutes of small talk, he told her, "You're too fat, Miss Gustafsson. You'll have to lose at least twenty pounds for the role I have in mind for you." Noticing the crushed look on Greta's face, Stiller's expression softened as he added, "I'll send for you in a few days for a screen test; then we'll see again."

After Greta had left, Stiller turned to actor Axel Nilsson, his friend and assistant, and said, "There's something quite extraordinary about that girl. I must discover what it is." The same day Stiller wrote in his diary: "I noticed at once how easily one can dominate her by looking straight into her eyes."

Some days later Stiller telephoned Greta and asked her to go for a screen test at Råsunda. She took a streetcar to the studio, trembling all the way with fright.

Once more Stiller let her wait for two hours before he showed up. When at last he did arrive he immediately had Greta sent to be made up. Her nerves were already close to the breaking point before she even came face to face with her tormentor.

One who had seen it all before was Julius Jaenzon, Stiller's cameraman. "He treats all newcomers this way," he told Greta reassuringly. "Don't let him frighten you. His bark is worse than his bite." He also told Greta something else, which gave her renewed courage and confidence: "You're the loveliest girl I've ever seen walk into this place."

Greta performed magnificently in front of the camera, and Stiller gave her the role for which he intended her from the start. His new film was *The Saga of Gösta Berling*, the story of a defrocked minister who becomes a tutor at the home of an aristocratic family, and falls in love with the Countess Elizabeth Dohna — played by Greta.

When Stiller introduced Greta to the executives of Svensk Filmindustri to discuss her contract, he told them: "You only get a face like that in front of a camera once in a century." Her contract was dated July 23, 1923, and had to be signed by her mother; Greta was still under age. Filming was estimated to take six months, for which she was to receive 3,000 kronor, or $600 in the currency of the period — about $5,000 today. Shooting started in September, when Greta was just eighteen.

For Mauritz Stiller there still remained one important problem: he wanted a shorter, more international-flavored name for his young protégée. Greta Gustafsson, he said, was fine for Sweden. But Stiller had his eye on the world.

Several people have laid claim to inventing the name Garbo; others have proffered explanations of its origin. Greta had already thought about changing her name while she was working at PUB and dreaming of a stage career. She did not think that Gustafsson was "refined" enough, she told Magdalena Hellberg. "She wanted a shorter name which could be pronounced easily in any language," Miss Hellberg recalled. "I remember her visiting some relatives from time to time who lived in Lidingö on a farm called 'Garboda.' It could be that she took the name Garbo from that."

Mimi Pollak claims that it was she who helped to invent the name after Stiller told Greta to think of some ideas. Wrote Mimi:

I had a friend, Oscar Adelssohn, who worked at the Ministry of Justice, and I took Greta to meet him. On the way to his office we thought of several names. I suggested "Garborn," and then we both

43

said at the same moment, "Why not Garbo?" Greta thought it was wonderful. "I won't even have to change the initials on my towels." Stiller liked the name, too.

The change was formally made on December 4, 1923. Three months later the name "Greta Garbo" made its debut in the screen credits of *The Saga of Gösta Berling*, which opened in Stockholm in March 1924.

Garbo herself remains evasive about the true origin of the name she made world-famous. When I told her the different versions I had heard and asked which was the real one, her answer was typical. "Anything is possible," was all she would say about the birth of Greta Garbo.

Chapter 3
STAR

The Divine
GARBO

Chapter 3
STAR

"Damn you, Stiller, I hate you!" Garbo shouted at her director in response to his relentless pressuring in a difficult scene during the filming of *The Saga of Gösta Berling.*

The young Garbo was now firmly in Stiller's hands, and the long and painful process of the making of a star had begun. It was the fall of 1923, and she was eighteen years old.

Stiller put his art before anything, and although he loved his protégée he would stop short of nothing to get the maximum performance from her. She later told an interviewer, "I enjoyed making the film, but it was like passing through a terrible fire." She was totally under Stiller's spell and obeyed him blindly. "She is like wax in my hands, and does everything I tell her," Stiller told a drama critic at the time. Garbo agreed; she told a Stockholm journalist, "Stiller creates people and shapes them according to his will." More than fifty years later she told me, "It was a love-hate affair; at times he loved me as much as I hated him."

What Stiller recognized in Garbo from the start was her exceptional ability to transform herself into any character, seeming actually to become that person for as long as need be. "All through the making of *Gösta Berling* (it took six months) I felt I was the Countess Elizabeth Dohna and lived nothing except the part," Garbo recalled later.

Following Stiller's advice, when filming was finished she returned to her classes at the Royal Dramatic Academy. *Gösta Berling* and her association with Stiller had increased her standing in the eyes of her fellow students. She was now a contract pupil, which meant an additional stipend and further opportunities to act in small parts in productions of the Royal Dramatic Theatre. Pleasant and unthreatening as the Academy was for Greta in such circumstances, it was a world she had already left behind. There was no doubt she would follow Stiller when his next call came.

If the Stockholm première of *Gösta Berling* — or Greta Garbo — failed to raise critics' enthusiasm, it did not dim Stiller's optimism for both the movie and his protégée. When Garbo's performance in the film was criticized, Stiller said, "She is still nervous and inexperienced, but there is something quite extraordinary about her. I am ruthless while breaking her in, but wait until I'm through. Then she will make the gods happy." The more he bullied her, the more often he made her cry, the closer Stiller came to succeeding in making her the greatest film actress the world has known.

Stiller's next project was cutting *Gösta Berling* into a shorter version for showing in the rest of Europe, with Berlin as his chief target. There he succeeded in selling the German rights to Trianon Films for 100,000 marks (then about $25,000) — a large amount for that time. In addition, he asked Trianon to pay his and Garbo's expenses for attending the Berlin première, and even obtained an advance of $1,000 to buy new clothes for her.

Unlike the Stockholm opening, the Berlin première in the fall of 1924 was an unqualified success. Rave notices applauded Garbo's "heartfelt" and "soul-revealing" performance. For the shy young star on her first visit abroad, the trip was an undreamed-of triumph. Later, in Hollywood, where she was uncomfortable with the American custom of casual embrace, she remembered the warmth of the German audiences: "They do not touch you," she explained, "yet they have their arms around you, always."

Soon afterward Stiller took Garbo back to Stockholm and started making plans for his next picture. Encouraged by the success of *Gösta Berling* — the film was breaking all records in Germany — Trianon offered Stiller even more money than before to make his next film for them. Stiller agreed to 150,000 marks for himself on condition that Trianon give Garbo a contract as well.

Trianon wanted him to make a movie based on a current best-selling novel whose plot centered around a luxury hotel in Germany. Stiller refused, arguing that he had already bought the screen rights to the story he wished to film, and if Trianon did not want it he would find backing elsewhere.

Called *The Odalisque from Smolny*, the memoirs of a White Russian refugee, the story had come to Stiller's attention many months before. It particularly appealed to him because he saw in it an ideal part for Garbo: an aristocratic Russian girl making her escape from a convent in Petrograd and fleeing to Constantinople — where she winds up in a harem.

Trianon was less than enthused, especially on hearing Stiller's plans for shooting the film on location in Constantinople. After weeks of haggling they gave their reluctant approval, if only to keep Stiller happy for another occasion.

Shortly before Christmas of 1924, an exuberant Stiller, with Garbo, actor Einar Hansson, and camera crew in tow, stepped aboard the *Orient Express*, headed for the Turkish capital. In Constantinople Stiller luxuriously installed himself and Garbo at the Pera Palace Hotel.

In no apparent hurry to start work, the party spent the days in leisurely shopping expeditions, sightseeing and leading the life of the idle rich. Stiller bought Garbo an expensive, ankle-length fur coat and valuable Oriental carpets for himself.

The first progress report that Trianon received from its prodigal director was a wire informing his producers that he had run out of money and asking for one million marks to be sent to him immediately. Receiving no response after two days, he wired again. When this also failed to bring a reply, the irate Stiller took a train to Berlin, leaving Garbo and the others in Constantinople to await his return. He could have saved himself the trouble had he known that Trianon had gone bankrupt and its directors were in jail. Penniless and stranded in a foreign country, Garbo, Hansson, and the crew of technicians had to be bailed out by the German and Swedish consulates and given tickets back to Berlin.

Undaunted by his Constantinople disaster, Stiller was already brimming with new ideas when Garbo arrived in Berlin. He was living imperially at the Esplanade, one of the city's most elegant hotels. He had not been in Berlin long enough to know that the whole of the German film industry had suffered a fate similar to Trianon's: overnight bankruptcy caused by crippling inflation.

But Stiller soon realized the situation and began making arrangements to return to Sweden with Garbo. At the same time, a little-known German director continued to look for Garbo. His wires sent to Stockholm and Constantinople had all been returned. He finally tracked her down in Berlin just as Stiller and she were about to leave.

Backed by American money and swimming against the tide, Georg W. Pabst was casting *Die Freudlose Gasse (The Street of Sorrow)*. He had seen *Gösta Berling* and badly wanted Garbo for his own film. Hard-pressed for money, Stiller accepted Pabst's offer for Garbo's services, but on his own terms. He appointed himself as "adviser" to his protégée, thus enabling him to stay on in Berlin during the shooting of the film. Garbo was paid $4,000 for the one month it took to make the movie.

What she and Stiller would do when it was finished was still anyone's guess.

The Street of Sorrow was the grim story of the decadence of Vienna after World War I — the epic of a people's struggle for survival amid hunger, squalor, and violence. Garbo gave a highly praised performance in the role of the elder daughter of a respected though impoverished family, which she tries to keep alive by turning to prostitution. Today the film ranks among the greatest in the annals of the cinema. It is also notable for the early film appearance of another European actress with "star quality": Marlene Dietrich.

Stiller and Garbo's extended stay in Berlin was to change their lives. In the spring of 1925 the czar of Hollywood, Louis B. Mayer, vice-president and production chief of Metro-Goldwyn-Mayer, was winding his way across Europe, meeting actors and directors and looking at new films. After Rome and Paris he was heading for Berlin.

Before leaving Hollywood Mayer had briefed himself carefully about everybody and everything worth seeing on the trip. Among those whose advice he sought was Victor Sjöström, the great Swedish director, who had left Sweden the year before and quickly made his mark in Hollywood. Sjöström urged Mayer to meet Stiller and to see *Gösta Berling*. Josef von Sternberg, another eminent European director, went a step further when he told Mayer to "import Stiller and include Greta Garbo in his luggage."

Arriving in Berlin, Mayer found Stiller shortly afterward at the Esplanade Hotel, and the two wasted little time in getting together. If the sharklike Hollywood tyrant expected to encounter another docile Swede, as he regarded the diplomatic Sjöström, he was wrong. When he met the tall, impressive Stiller he saw a confident man extravagantly and elegantly dressed, with nothing in his manner that betrayed his recent setbacks.

The appointment had been made by intermediaries, and

it was not until the two men came face to face that they discovered they could not converse: neither spoke the other's language. Each had a smattering of Yiddish, but not enough, and an interpreter had to be sent for.

While waiting for the interpreter to arrive, Mayer managed to make himself sufficiently understood to tell Stiller that he wanted to see *Gösta Berling* as soon as possible, as his stay in Berlin would be short. Stiller had access to a screening room belonging to Ufa-Film at the Potsdammerplatz, not far from his hotel. He had a print of the film in his room, so as soon as the interpreter arrived, they could immediately hold an impromptu screening.

At one point during the showing Mayer asked a question through the interpreter, but Stiller motioned him to be quiet. After that the men watched in silence. When it was over and the lights went up, the usually noncommittal Mayer beamed with delight and slapped Stiller on the back repeatedly to show his pleasure and admiration. At the same time he was saying something that Stiller could not understand.

Addressing himself to the interpreter, Mayer said, "Tell Mr. Stiller that a man of his talents should be in Hollywood." Noticing Stiller's blank expression, Mayer continued, "Tell him that I will sign him for three years and pay him $1,500 a week for a start."

As they sauntered down the street, Mayer waited for Stiller to respond to the offer he had made him. When Stiller finally spoke, he asked, "What about Greta Garbo? You have not mentioned her."

"What about her?" retorted Mayer, taken aback by the unexpected question. "Who is this Garbo?" he asked with clear lack of interest. Although he had been impressed by her performance, his mind was not on Garbo but on the talented director. When Stiller finished extolling Garbo's virtues, Mayer said, "Then I should meet her at least," but added quickly, "more important is how soon you can come to Hollywood."

Rapport between the two was not made easier by the need for an interpreter, and Stiller was getting impatient. Now he came straight to the point: "I will go to America only if Miss Garbo goes with me and is put under contract as well," he said adamantly. This was more than Mayer was prepared for, and he told Stiller so. He would, however, think about it, he said. Before they parted, Mayer accepted Stiller's invitation for dinner the next day, when he would meet Garbo and they could talk about it again.

Stiller prepared for the occasion with special care. To play host to filmland's most powerful man he ordered a superb meal in advance, starting with caviar, and chose the best table in the Esplanade's decorous, chandelier-lit restaurant. He coached Garbo in making a carefully timed entrance and also in everything she was to say. The theme throughout was: "Mr. Stiller knows what is best for me. I always do what Mr. Stiller says."

He might as well not have troubled. Mayer paid only scant attention to her beauty while engrossed in conversation with Stiller.

Before the evening ended Mayer agreed to sign Garbo to a three-year contract at $350 a week for the first year, increasing to $750 by the third. He let Stiller know that it was only for his sake that he met his demands concerning Garbo.

When all business was settled, Mayer, with a nod toward Garbo, instructed the interpreter, "Tell her that in America men don't like fat women." On hearing the interpreter's translation, Garbo rose slowly from her chair, head and shoulders held high, and made a dignified exit.

Although she disliked the squat, unpolished Mayer, she quickly forgot his quip about fat women and looked forward with intense excitement to her visit to America. It was still two months before departure, and she would go on a strict diet.

HOLLYWOOD

The Divine GARBO

HOLLYWOOD

At the end of June 1925 Garbo's family saw her off on the first stage of the long journey to California. Five years later she recalled for a Swedish biography, *Greta Garbos Saga*,

My mother, my brother, and my sister were together with me at the Central Station in Stockholm when I left for the ship to New York. My mother's eyes were swollen with tears, but she did everything to look happy. "Mother, I will be back in one year," I said. "One year, that is only twelve months. It will pass very soon." But it took three and a half years before I came back to Sweden.

Greta Garbo and Mauritz Stiller were in high spirits when they boarded the Swedish liner *Drottningholm* at Gothenburg. The newly acclaimed star of two highly praised movies and the famous European film director were on their way to conquer America, and they celebrated their good fortune during the ten-day voyage across the Atlantic. In New York a welcoming committee of studio heads would be waiting at the dock bearing bouquets of flowers. Photographers would scramble for position as Garbo stepped off the boat. Stiller had coached her for the occasion during the trip. She would tell the reporters, "This is the happiest moment of my life. God bless America."

The dream turned into a nightmare. Their high hopes were shattered instantly upon arrival, and all that awaited them were heartbreaks and humiliation.

A solitary photographer came aboard to take some routine poses of the two leaning against the ship's railing. M-G-M sent a publicity department junior and an interpreter to drive them to their downtown hotel. There was not a flower in sight.

As Garbo's eyes filled with tears, Stiller consoled her, "Wait until we get to Hollywood in a few days. Everything will be different." He could not have known that the "few days" would turn into months, that it would be half a year before Greta Garbo was given her first role in a film, and that he himself, blacklisted and driven from Hollywood, would be dead within three years.

New York was having one of its hottest spells on record during the two months M-G-M abandoned them there before anyone moved to bring them to the Coast or find them work. Garbo spent most of the time cooling off in her bath at the Hotel Commodore while Stiller made fruitless efforts to reach M-G-M executives. He found it impossible to get through to Louis B. Mayer. Each time he called the studios he was told, "Mr. Mayer is in conference. Leave your number and we'll call you back." But Mayer never called back.

His patience exhausted, Stiller went to the Swedish consulate and found someone to write a letter for him in English, telling Mayer that he wished to break his and Garbo's contracts and return to Sweden. Even that failed to bring a response. For Stiller, a celebrity in his own right, this was the ultimate humiliation.

Garbo described those two months in New York as "the most miserable period of my career." In a letter to a friend in Stockholm, she wrote, "I feel suicidal. I will either drown myself in the bath or jump out of the window, but I lack the courage and may take the next boat home. Everything is in a mess."

M-G-M continued to debate what to do with them. Through his daily calls and letters, Stiller was soon labeled an "interfering nuisance" at the studio. Keeping the pair at length was thought preferable to having them sit on M-G-M's doorstep. "After all, they're paid," was the general attitude of studio heads.

Finally, Garbo and Stiller, at the end of their tether, set out from their hotel to pay a call at the office of the Swedish-American Line to inquire about sailings home. It was to prove their first piece of luck since their arrival, and it came from the least expected quarter.

Martha Hedman, a Swedish singer at the Metropolitan Opera, was at the shipping office that day making arrangements about going to Sweden on holiday. She and Stiller were old friends and happy to meet again. They agreed to have lunch together, and Stiller told Martha Hedman about Garbo and the story of their plight.

Miss Hedman was sure she could help. She would take them to the studio of her friend, the famous photographer Arnold Genthe. Genthe's memoirs record the encounter. He was struck instantly by Garbo's unique features and exceptional beauty. Garbo looked admiringly at the pile of photos on Genthe's desk and told him, "I would love you to take some pictures of me sometime."

"Why sometime? Why not now?" Genthe asked her. "You're here and I'm here."

Garbo protested shyly, "Not now, please. Look at my hair and dress."

"Never mind about that," said Genthe, "I'm more interested in your eyes and what's behind that extraordinary forehead."

Seeing that Genthe could prove invaluable to them, Stiller told Garbo to go ahead. For the next hour she obeyed Genthe's instructions while the photographer, taking mostly close-ups, brought out the full depth of her beauty from a variety of carefully chosen angles, making maximum use of light and shadows.

When the pictures were ready, Genthe and Stiller together selected the best of them. The renowned photographer took them personally to show to editors of the leading magazines. *Vanity Fair* chose the most beautiful, a portrait in which she is resting her chin on her hand, and introduced it with the headline, "A NEW STAR FROM THE NORTH — GRETA GARBO." The accompanying copy read:

Greta Garbo is the latest adjunct to the Swedish film colony in Hollywood, which includes Victor Seastrom and Benjamin Christianson. . . . She was offered an opportunity to play the lead in *The Story of Gösta Berling*. . . . This Miss Garbo, aged nineteen, revealed such fine dramatic instincts that many continental film companies bid high for her.

Stiller sent a set of the Genthe prints to his friend Victor Sjöström in California. As soon as Sjöström received them, he took the photographs to Mayer and spread them out in front of him on his desk. Mayer was spellbound. "Who is she? Go get her at once!" he said. When he was told it was Greta Garbo, whom he had all but forgotten, Mayer refused to believe that this was the same girl he had met in Berlin a mere few months before. Sjöström reminded him that Garbo and Stiller had been in New York since July, awaiting instructions to come to Hollywood. Mayer invited them to the Coast forthwith, and Sjöström telephoned Stiller in New York to give him the news.

There is a story that Garbo's picture appeared on the cover of *Vanity Fair* during the six-day train journey to Los Angeles and caught the attention of M-G-M executives. They immediately ordered their underlings to track her down and sign her, and were considerably embarrassed when it was discovered that she was already under contract to them.

It was early September when Garbo and Stiller arrived at the Los Angeles railroad station. This time a real welcoming committee awaited them, headed by Victor Sjöström and members of the Swedish colony, as well as several reporters and photographers. Garbo was smothered in flowers as she stepped off the train wearing a light blouse and long skirt. A little Swedish girl in national costume handed a large bouquet to the smiling and confused Greta as the cameras clicked. She was barraged by questions fired at her in a language she did not speak. Through an interpreter sent by the studio, she answered as best she could. Finally, a reporter asked in German, "What are your plans, Miss Garbo?" She told him, "I wait for what the studio decides to do with me." For good measure she threw in the English lines she had rehearsed before arriving in New York: "This is the happiest moment of my life. God bless America."

But in the reports of her arrival the press was not as generous. One reporter had asked where she would stay in Hollywood; through the interpreter she had replied that she was looking for something not too expensive, preferably a room with a "nice private family." Her naïveté was mocked in the columns, which were certainly less than kind. A run in her stocking, her shoes that needed new heels, her unbecoming hairstyle, were all gleefully noted. One writer even made the unlikely claim that she had helped Garbo unpack and thus was able to inform her readers that the new star wore cotton underwear. Garbo's Stockholm roots were regarded as laughable, and one columnist suggested she be sent back to "Swedish Brooklyn" without delay. The overriding question was, what on earth did Stiller see in her?

M-G-M had rented a small house for Stiller in Santa Monica and an apartment for Garbo at the nearby Hotel Miramar.

Stiller's house had a pool and garden where Garbo spent most of the time swimming and sunbathing. She enjoyed her new surroundings, and began to shed the melancholy from which she suffered since arriving in New York. Most of all, both were looking forward to start work.

But the days passed and the studio maintained a marked silence. Homesick and lonely, knowing little English, Garbo took some comfort from her correspondence with Lars Saxon, a friend in Stockholm whom she had met through Vera Schmiterlöw. Over the next three years, between her arrival in the United States and her first return to Sweden after what seemed to her an exile, she wrote him long letters and was grateful for his replies. Five weeks after her arrival in California, she wrote:

If you would know how happy your letters made me and how they took me back home. You're quite right when you think I don't feel at home here. I'm dreaming of the theaters which are open there now. Oh you lovely little Sweden, I promise that when I return to you my sad face will smile as never before.

I haven't been out to any entertainments since I arrived. I go to bed as early as possible, and don't do anything during the day. I have not started work yet. It seems to me it will take time, and I am sad to say that I'm not sorry. Neither am I sorry about my retiring life. I don't care if I act like a little old woman.

Garbo was twenty.

Stiller too fell back into moods of depression. His only friend in the M-G-M hierarchy was still Victor Sjöström, and it was to him that Stiller turned in his renewed despair. Sjöström, remembering Mayer's burst of enthusiasm when he had been shown Genthe's photographs of Garbo, was equally baffled by the studio's subsequent lack of interest once she was there. Now he could do only one more thing for his sorely tried friend and compatriot: he would take him personally to Irving Thalberg.

Thalberg was M-G-M's undisputed "boy wonder." At twenty-six he had risen from office boy to production manager, becoming the most powerful man in the organization after Mayer. For a man known for his fiery temperament, Thalberg showed unusual restraint on meeting the haughty Stiller. Sjöström played the role of interpreter, and if the half-hour encounter ended cordially and with promises of early action, it was thanks to his quickness in changing Stiller's often pompous utterances into congenial-sounding and reasonable conversation. The meeting ended with Thalberg agreeing to giving Garbo a new screen test under Stiller's personal direction and supervision.

The result of the test was electrifying. It impressed Mayer, Thalberg, and every executive who saw it. It was rerun eight times in succession, as the news spread. Immediately the studio went into action. Scenario department heads stayed the night combing their files for a suitable story. The next day Garbo herself started being remolded. Mayer ordered her teeth perfected, saying there was too much space between them. He also demanded that she lose more weight before filming began. Dressers set to work on her hair.

It was not easy for the script department to find a story suited to Garbo's broad-shouldered stature, which was considered "unusual" by conventional Hollywood standards — female stars were generally petite, and glamour was the order of the day. And in fact, the script department was not responsible for Garbo's first M-G-M role. It is not altogether clear who was.

Filming of *The Torrent*, directed by Monta Bell, had just started when Alma Rubens, playing the lead role of Leonora opposite Ricardo Cortez, was taken sick. Bell heard the news from his assistant as they walked to a projection room to look at rushes of some flood scenes. But instead of seeing flood scenes, they found themselves staring at Greta Garbo, whose screen test had inexplicably been mixed up with the rushes.

The projectionist, realizing the mistake, stopped the test to change the film, but Bell called to him to let it run. When it came to the end, Bell asked to see it once more. Then he climbed into the projection room to look at the can and its label. It read: "Greta Garbo (Swedish actress)" and the date of the test.

Seized with excitement, Bell rushed out in search of Irving Thalberg. When he finally found him he was still gasping for breath as he told him about the test he had just seen. "I want that girl for *The Torrent!*" he spluttered. On learning that Alma Rubens had dropped out, Thalberg agreed to replace her with Garbo.

Greta was elated when she heard the news — but not for long. It had not entered her mind that she could be assigned to a film of which Stiller was not in charge. Once the truth sunk in, she threatened to refuse the part and go home. Stiller decided otherwise. However great his humiliation, he would rehearse his protégée each evening for her next day's scenes. Soon after shooting began, Stiller wrote to Axel Nilsson: "Greta is starting to work with a well-known movie director, and it is my opinion that she has an excellent part. If she only has energy, she is going to earn millions here."

When Mayer heard of Stiller's secret coaching of Garbo, he went to look at the rushes. Enthralled by what he saw, he sent for Stiller and told him, "If she is a success I'll let you direct her next picture. I'll also give you the finest watch you ever saw."

During the shooting the press continued to comment on "Stiller's Folly." According to one columnist, "this peasant girl with the big feet" was the laughingstock of the lot. Walter Winchell was not the only one to advance the big feet rumor, which of course stayed with her for years. A reporter claimed to have discovered her shoe size (a whopping eight, he trumpeted) when he pursued her into a shoe store. Even if Garbo could not or chose not to read these reports, she still suffered

61

from them as crew and actors on the set of *The Torrent* repeated them in her presence. She was learning to understand English quickly, more quickly than her co-workers realized, but had no defense other than a blank stare when she heard herself called "Super Svenska" and "The Skyscraper."

It is hard to know why in those early days the press so disliked her, except that a bandwagon of criticism makes clever copy and is easy to join. Surely some of the comments were patently ridiculous, such as the report, seriously made, that her face was so asymmetrical that she had to be shot in three-quarter profile whenever possible. William Daniels was assigned to photograph *The Torrent*, and he remembers his first meeting with Garbo. One Sunday morning the studio called him in to run tests. He was never happy about working on Sunday, but he did as he was told. When he arrived, there was Garbo, withdrawn and frightened. "She couldn't speak a word of English," Daniels recalled. He saw at once how very young and horribly shy she was, a foreigner among people she could not understand. Daniels felt sorry for her. "It must have been a horrifying experience," he said.

Daniels, a kind man and brilliant photographer, concentrated on gaining her confidence as he worked. His job was to find his subject's best features and enhance them, and he was immediately struck by Garbo's eyes. Over the years, from *The Torrent* to *Ninotchka*, Daniels would photograph all but four of Garbo's films; in each of them he continued to explore and reveal with his camera the mystery and beauty of Garbo's eyes. On that first day, he noted that she photographed best from the left, but from any angle her face was magnificent. Unlike most stars, he realized, Garbo simply had no "bad angles"; her facial planes were nearly perfect.

Production of *The Torrent* took only six weeks, a not uncommon schedule then. The results of Stiller's coaching and his unique understanding of his actress were apparent in Garbo's performance. The film premiered in New York on February 21, 1926; the week before, a worried and insecure Garbo had written to Saxon:

Had a talk with the manager of M-G-M yesterday. He was angry because he thinks I worry unnecessarily about everything. I couldn't speak to him — it was like talking to a wall. We are too different. I was very unhappy. Again and again I get frightening thoughts about the future.

The Torrent was breaking box-office records at New York's Capitol Theatre by the second week of its run. The picture's special effects were lavish. The "torrent" itself, a spectacular cloudburst in which an entire village was demolished, was a feat involving tons of water and the best efforts of M-G-M's engineering department; it received almost as much comment as the appearance of the new star. Garbo was well received: she was described as "young, slim, with strange, haunting eyes"; the Brooklyn *Eagle* commented, "Miss Garbo is not beautiful, but she is a brilliant actress." Columnists took another look at Garbo — the awkward girl in the "funny checked suit" who had arrived on Hollywood's doorstep in November was now "a comet appearing in the Northern sky." Apparently they had read the reviews:

She registers a complete success. She is not so much an actress as she is endowed with individuality and magnetism. [*Motion Picture*]

This girl has everything, with looks, acting ability, and personality. [*Variety*]

And on February 29 the girl with everything wrote to her friend at home in Stockholm:

During last week I haven't met one Swede, and was all alone every evening. I wasn't even sorry about it. I'm getting used to it now.

Who knows, maybe I'll end up on some uninhabited island one day to avoid people. . . .

If you call my sister don't forget to tell her that I'll be coming home quite soon. Tell her also that she can be happy to be living in Sweden and shouldn't think that everywhere else is Paradise.

Certainly Garbo did not find America to be paradise. In the fall of 1925, shortly after her arrival in California, she had written to Saxon:

It could be so beautiful here if the Americans themselves had not made it so ugly with their big buildings, the millions of cars, and noise, but I have retired to the most quiet place where you don't see any films or anything else.

The studios are hideous and everything is crowded — just like my head sometimes.

She found herself very much a stranger in a strange land, and her letters to Saxon continued to reflect her alienation and confusion. "It is bitter to think of one's best years disappearing in this unpolished country" (February 5, 1926). "Americans don't understand anything about us Europeans" (July 6, 1926). "The people here are incapable of feeling deeply about anything, according to my experience. Perhaps it is different in other parts of America, but I haven't found any sign of it" (January 30, 1927). Most succinctly, on August 20, 1927, she wrote: "I'm tired and nervous and I'm in America. Here you don't know that you live."

But after *The Torrent* the die was cast, and for the next fifteen years — until the resounding failure of *Two-Faced Woman* in 1941, twenty-three movies later, which ended her career — she lived in Hollywood, perhaps its ultimate creation and captive.

Garbo with Frederick Sands at Lake Davos, Switzerland, 1977

Karl Gustafsson (second from right) at work

Garbo and Vera Schmiterlöw advertising the 1923 Lancia Lambda

Garbo in the dress given
her by Gösta Kyhlberg

Filming *The Saga of Gösta Berling:* from left Julius Jaenzon, cameraman; Mauritz Stiller, director; Barascutti, lights; G. Ramsten, wigmaker; Mona Mårtenson, Lars Hanson, Garbo, actors

Garbo in *The Street of Sorrow*, 1925

Garbo in Berlin, 1925

Garbo in *The Torrent*, 1926

Garbo and Stiller arriving
in New York on the
Drottningholm, July 1925

Arnold Genthe's *Vanity
Fair* cover photograph of
Garbo, 1925

The Garbo feet as seen in a publicity still for *Love*, 1927

Garbo's reunion with her ▶ mother on the train to Stockholm, December 1928

Garbo and John Gilbert in *Flesh and the Devil*, 1927

Garbo and Nils Asther in *The Single Standard*, 1929

Garbo on a day off, Hollywood, 1929

Garbo on board the *Kungsholm* on her way to Sweden, 1935

The Temptress, 1926

Riding on the crest of Garbo's successful American debut in *The Torrent*, M-G-M quickly announced her next movie, *The Temptress* — with Mauritz Stiller, Garbo's discoverer, mentor, and friend, as director.

The appointment of Stiller was a disaster, and the atmosphere surrounding *The Temptress* was tense even before filming began. Stiller had written the script, based, like *The Torrent*, on a Blasco-Ibáñez novel, and both Mayer and Thalberg liked it. But it had to be translated, and Stiller believed the translation "mutilated" his work. He was furious, reacting violently and throwing tantrums that were too much for the executives to take seriously. Shooting had barely started under his direction when the first rows broke out, stirred up by his antagonistic manner and ignorance of American moviemaking. When he saw some fifty people standing on the set the first morning, he demanded to know what they were doing there. Told that they were assistant directors, production assistants, stand-ins, and so on, he ordered them all to leave. "Camera and actors is all I need," he announced. His lack of English compounded the situation: he made himself the laughingstock of all by his bellowed instructions to the cameraman to "stop" when he meant "go," by shouting at extras to "explode" when he wanted them to applaud. The leading man, Antonio Moreno, was not spared his outbursts: Stiller insisted, unsuccessfully, that the handsome Latin-style lover shave off his prized moustache. For Garbo herself, confused and unhappy because of the constant commotion and unpleasantness on the set, worse was to come. In the first week of shooting she was handed a wire informing her of the sudden death in Stockholm of her sister, Alva.

After two weeks of total havoc on the set of *The Temptress*, Stiller was dismissed by Thalberg, who told him, "Get out and never show your face here again." Garbo later told an interviewer that on hearing Stiller would not be allowed to finish the picture, "I was broken to pieces, nobody knows."

Stiller, she explained, was an artistic creator, accustomed to the European style of filmmaking in which he alone as director made all decisions. He simply could not understand the American way of making pictures, which Garbo called "factories." He was replaced by Fred Niblo, who was left with most of the film to complete. Garbo wrote to Saxon:

Stiller retired from my film because he couldn't work together with the others. That was a hard time, too. I was so exhausted that I didn't know what to do anymore. Then we got another director, who asked me all the time if I was "happy." After everything which happened before, this was a little nerve-racking.

Still, Garbo recognized and appreciated Niblo's concern and professionalism. She gave him a signed photograph inscribed, "To Fred Niblo with a piece of my heart."

When Garbo had read the news of her sister's death she had collapsed and had to be taken home. That shock, Stiller's disgrace, and the difficulties of filming *The Temptress* drained and depressed her. She tried to express her feelings in a letter to Saxon:

I have been unhappy to be so far from my own people and without being able to do something for them. I won't talk about what I have been through, except it would have been easier for me if I could have been with them, who have suffered as I did. I have become afraid of life.

The shocks in life can make you frightened, and I don't understand why God suddenly hurt me so deeply. It is as if somebody cut away a piece from my inside. I always wonder if something has changed my life, but don't know what it is.

Still, she tried to be optimistic:

I still hope that there will be some happiness for me in the future. . . .

I have tried to be able to go home, but everybody advised against it. They say that if I go too soon, I'll ruin everything for myself here. I suppose they know best and say that until I have made three films I shouldn't think of leaving. Perhaps it will take another six months, but then I have to go. It will be melancholic, strange, and wonderful. Is there anything better than to be longing for something, when you know it is within reach?

But home, family, Sweden, were not within reach. In the fall of 1926 she reported to Saxon:

I've worked 5–6 months on my second film [*The Temptress*] until a week ago — and am now going to be thrown straight into another.

I'm so sick and tired of everything, all I want is to run away. I've had trouble with Metro-Goldwyn, been forced to turn to the manager and tried to talk with him, although I don't know anything about how to run the business.

I've become so nervous that one day I will make a scandal and leave everything. If you knew how hard you have to work here, it is beyond one's power. . . .

I hope I will be rewarded for all the years I have sacrificed for money. My God, imagine to go back home when the time here is over — and in addition somewhat wealthy. How good it would be. But no increase of salary yet. Those greedy people!

The Temptress opened in New York on October 10, 1926. This time reviewers remembered only Garbo: nothing else in the film mattered. The vamp image, which M-G-M of course was happy to promote, was perceived: one reviewer warned that viewing Garbo in action would make husbands look askance at their wives. After *The Temptress* was released, fan mail addressed simply to "Greta Garbo, Hollywood, California" began pouring in to M-G-M. She soon stopped reading any of it, shocked by the amount of pornography her overwrought public was writing, and sent all letters back to the publicity department unopened. From serious critics she drew a chorus of acclaim for her acting, her beauty, and her poise. And indeed, as Elena, the siren wife of a weak South American, Garbo glowed with passion each time she appeared on the screen. Her beauty sparked with a unique appeal. Only the actress was dissatisfied with her work. She wrote to Saxon:

The Temptress has now been shown here — terrible. The story, Garbo, everything is extremely bad. It is no exaggeration to say that I was dreadful. I was tired, couldn't sleep and everything went wrong. But the main reason is, I suppose, that I'm no actress.

"I know nothing of the technique of acting," Garbo declared later, adding, "For the time being I felt I actually *was* the person I played. I don't know how I got certain effects or why I did things the way I did."

Nils Asther, her Swedish co-star in *Wild Orchids*, remembered years later, "I used to stand behind the camera and watch her act. Her motions and gestures seemed ungainly and crude, but when seen on film they were marvelous."

Directors liked to work with Garbo because they could count on her to have worked on her lines and know them — and those of the other actors appearing with her — perfectly before each scene. Because of her careful preparations it was seldom necessary to do retakes, which saved the studio costly shooting time and enabled directors to bring in Garbo films more quickly than other similar productions. Clarence Brown, who directed Garbo in seven pictures, including *Flesh and the Devil* and *Anna Christie*, recalled, "We had to place screens — called 'flats' — around the set when she acted, because if she saw other people looking at her she would get flustered. In silent days lights were so bright that she could not see off the set. When sound came in, new lights were used and were dim enough so she could see everybody around. The sight of an

68

electrician or carpenter would put her off balance. But she was the best in the world to handle as an actress. I loved her and loved to work with her."

Ernst Lubitsch, who directed Garbo in *Ninotchka*, remembered that Garbo did not suffer from a "slavish devotion to the mirror," a common failing of women stars. "They are so much concerned about their looks that they exhaust their vitality before they start," he said. Lubitsch also described Garbo as "probably the most inhibited person I have ever worked with. When you finally break through this, and she really feels a scene, she's wonderful. But if you don't succeed in making her feel it, she can't do it cold-bloodedly on technique alone."

But in the end, of course, none of the analyses mattered. Lewis Stone, who acted with her in seven movies, put it best: "She was Greta Garbo, and that said it all. No one ever created such an impression."

The Temptress made Garbo a valuable Hollywood property to be actively promoted. M-G-M's publicity department was ordered to create an image for Garbo that would add her to the pantheon of world-famous *femmes fatales*, and took a series of stills in which she is seen dripping in furs, reclining seductively on couches, and in similar "Eternal Woman" poses. The newspapers were cooperative: when it ran one of these vamp pictures in 1926, the Brooklyn *Eagle* asked its readers, "Do you think soulful-eyed Greta Garbo resembles Pola Negri? She's supposed to."

Then, in an apparent attempt to demonstrate her versatility, the publicity department announced that the "Stockholm Venus" was also the healthy outdoors type, and posed her in athletic shorts with the University of Southern California track team. To make studio identification complete, there is Garbo sharing the camera with an embodiment of Leo, the M-G-M trademark. Somehow she manages to retain her dignity: even in these perfectly dreadful pictures she wears a slightly bemused expression that seems to convey the message that she is not taking any of this too seriously. She was still mystified by the process of Hollywood star-making, but even when forced into ridiculous situations she remained true to herself.

Garbo was also encouraged to give interviews in which she recited answers written out for her by the publicity department to questions the publicity department had briefed the reporters to ask. Yes, she said, it was true that she preferred moustached to clean-shaven men to play her lovers. How did she care for that flawless complexion? She scrubbed it every day with plain soap, water, and a good stiff brush.

Unsure of her position at the studio and wanting to cooperate and succeed, Garbo complied readily, if not happily, in this campaign. Indeed, her willingness made her known as the darling of the publicity department. Only when Harry Edington began to represent her did she decline such exploitation. Realizing that his client was cut out of different and finer stuff than Hollywood was used to, he encouraged her to refuse silly publicity photos and insipid interviews. His boldest stroke was the simplest and most telling: he made it clear that she was to be referred to by surname alone. She was to be simply, and completely, Garbo. The star had been born; this, perhaps, was the birth of the legend.

Garbo's third American movie was *Flesh and the Devil*, made in 1926. She had been given the script immediately after completing *The Temptress*. She didn't like it, regarding her role as just one more "silly temptress" who got all dressed up and took pleasure in destroying men. She felt her career was in danger as she saw herself playing one dreary vamp after another. Louis B. Mayer heard of her displeasure and called her to his office. He informed her that there would be no arguments: she would start filming right away, and that was that. Garbo recalled the meeting in her last Hollywood interview, given in 1928 to Ruth Biery of *Photoplay:* " 'Meester Mayer,' I said, for I could not then talk but a little English and not so good pronunciation, 'I am sick. I cannot do another picture right away. And I am also unhappy about this picture.' And he said, 'That is just too bad.' What I wouldn't have given to be born an American girl, to have understood the American language and the American business."

So *Flesh and the Devil* went into production, with the dashing John Gilbert playing opposite the twenty-one-year-old Garbo. William Daniels was again cameraman, and he convinced director Clarence Brown to use extreme close-ups. Brown resisted at first, but when he saw the astonishing impact of Garbo's face filling the screen, he realized Daniels was right. When the movie premiered in New York on January 9, 1927, the New York *Herald Tribune* declared, "Never before has a woman so alluring, with a seductive grace that is far more potent than mere beauty, appeared on the screen. . . . Never in our screen career have we seen seduction so perfectly done." The offscreen love affair between Garbo and Gilbert, heavily publicized by M-G-M, delighted the public and drew audiences. Although it was said that Mayer personally disliked the picture, he was surely happy about its success at the box office. He also must have observed that Garbo was the first female star to draw huge numbers of her own sex to the movies. The majority of filmgoers were women, and they could be counted on to come out to see a favorite male star. Now they were flocking to the theaters to gaze upon a woman's face, which they watched not so much in envy as in awe. Throughout her career Garbo would appeal to women as strongly as to men.

After *Flesh and the Devil*, M-G-M cast Garbo in *Women Love Diamonds*. When she read the script and discovered that she was to portray yet another seductress, she told Mayer she would play no more "bad womens," and refused to come to the studio for costume fittings. Mayer informed her by letter that she was breaking her contract. Money was also an issue: during *Flesh and the Devil* Garbo was still being paid only $600 a week, while Gilbert's weekly check was $10,000. In November she brought the matter to a head by going to Mayer and demanding that her salary be raised to $5,000. When Mayer offered her half that, Garbo told him, "I tank I go home now," and left. She stayed away for seven months, during which time of course she received no salary at all. She wrote to Saxon:

I saw in the newspapers from home that I get paid $5,000 a week. Unusually admirable! Perhaps I would forgive myself for being here if I would get that much. I wonder what they would say if they knew that I haven't been paid for more than four months.

The press was divided in its coverage of the long dispute: refusal of a role by an actor under contract was unheard of in Hollywood. Some of the columnists regarded Garbo as temperamental and a troublemaker; others saw a brave star pitted against the M-G-M colossus.

Gilbert supported Garbo, and advised her to see Harry Edington, Hollywood's leading business manager, who had successfully negotiated Gilbert's own million-dollar contract. After one look at Garbo, Edington lost no time in taking her contract to M-G-M, threatening to tear it up unless it was replaced by a new one for five years, starting at $5,000. Additionally, he took the view that since Garbo was expected to be available for work all year round, there was no justification for not paying her fifty-two weeks of the year. This was revolutionary: until then it had been normal practice for artists to be paid only forty weeks' salary a year. Edington also tactfully persuaded Mayer to give Pauline Stark the leading role in *Women Love Diamonds*, and to cast Garbo in *Love*, a watered-down version of Tolstoy's *Anna Karenina*, in which her character, though an adulteress, was developed and sympathetic.

Finally Mayer, not unaware of how much money Garbo's films were grossing around the world, agreed to meet Edington's terms.

Garbo's new contract was finally negotiated in June 1927 — the same month a defeated Stiller left Hollywood. After the fiasco of *The Temptress*, it was clear he would never work for M-G-M again. He directed *Hotel Imperial* with Pola Negri for Paramount. The film was well received and, encouraged by its success, Paramount gave him two more pictures to direct. Both failed. His hopes revived briefly when M-G-M announced plans for Garbo to star in *The Divine Woman*, to be based on a play about Sarah Bernhardt. Pocketing his pride, Stiller went to see Mayer, telling him that this was the one film he should be allowed to direct. But Mayer would have nothing more to do with him, and neither would any other studio in Hollywood. In poor health and broken in spirit, Stiller went back to Sweden. Garbo saw him off in Los Angeles, and they wept bitterly. She never saw him again.

After Stiller left Hollywood, Garbo made five films in rapid succession — *Love* ("I am the mother of an eleven-year-old son — funny, what?"), *The Divine Woman*, *The Mysterious Lady*, *A Woman of Affairs*, and *Wild Orchids*. All the prints of *The Divine Woman*, released in January 1928, have been lost, but the surviving stills show a new warmth and openness to her features. Her relaxed expression may reflect the confidence she enjoyed working with her friend and countryman, Victor Sjöström, who directed. *The Mysterious Lady*, in which she played a Russian spy called Tania Federova, was the best of a stack of scripts about unfaithful wives, divas, sirens, and assorted fallen women that M-G-M had considered for her sixth film. Then, in *A Woman of Affairs*, based loosely on Michael Arlen's scandalous and popular novel *The Green Hat*, she again played an adulteress, and in the final scene kills herself by driving her elegant car into a tree. Garbo was one of the few female stars whose fans would tolerate her screen death again and again; others were never allowed to be dispatched as often as she was.

Although she was busy, successful, and well paid, her homesickness continued. In August 1927 she wrote to Saxon, "Next year I can go home for a visit, and I think it is the only thing that can cheer me up. I'm longing so very much for dear old Sweden." But in December she wrote in disappointment:

I have asked and begged to go home for Christmas, but you cannot talk to these people here. My head is spinning when I think of the wonderful time you will all have at home. And I will be here alone. It's not pleasant. Oh, if I could come to your house and have coffee by the window and look out on the snow and the water. But there will come one day. . . .

Whether I work or not I am tired and unhappy and don't want to do anything. I don't go anywhere and just sit down staring. I will soon become a little old woman if I continue like this. I live like I was seventy years old.

Still in Hollywood, she gave an interview — a rare one — to Swedish journalist Leonard Clairmont, who got his story but not without some embarrassment. He told Sven Broman,

When I got the interview with Garbo all the other reporters were very jealous. I asked her if she intended to visit Sweden that year, 1928. I knew that she had promised her mother to come, but had postponed her trip several times. "Yes," Garbo said, "I shall visit my mother this Christmas."

"Look into my eyes and swear to go," I insisted.

"I have promised my mother, and I am going to keep my promise," she said. A photographer took a picture just as we shook hands on that.

My interview, headlined "GARBO LOVAR" ("GARBO PROMISES"), was published in a Swedish weekly. It was translated and published in a Norwegian weekly as well; the Norwegian headline was "GARBO LOVER." The photograph appeared in both.

74

M-G-M's publicity people saw the Norwegian paper and demanded an explanation. What the hell did I mean by calling myself Garbo's lover?

It took me a while to convince them that "lover" meant something else in Norwegian!

In August 1928 she wrote to Saxon, "I am presently working like mad on a new film, A Woman of Affairs. Immediately afterwards I am leaving the 'factory' — with or without permission." But immediately after A Woman of Affairs came Wild Orchids.

Garbo was glad enough to follow Edington's advice and refuse interviews, and her refusal had inflamed many columnists, who resumed their attacks. Once again she was being criticized for her height, her wide shoulders, her awkwardness, her lack of "oomph"; she was called "Miss Human Ice Cream." She did not look like a star, and she was certainly not behaving like a star. She was undeniably successful, yet reluctant to revel in her success in ways Hollywood understood and expected. Harry Edington, concerned about the wave of unpleasant stories, prevailed on Garbo to agree to a long and serious interview with Ruth Biery of Photoplay. The story ran in three installments, in April, May, and June of 1928. Then almost twenty-three years old, Garbo had completed five films for M-G-M (she had just finished The Divine Woman). Her English was clear and competent, and she no longer required an interpreter.

She spoke of a great loneliness for her family, especially her father: "My father died when I was fourteen. God, what a feeling. Someone you love is there, then he is not there." She remembered herself in adolescence as "so big, so very big"; she had attained her full height by the time she was twelve. Of her dramatic training in Stockholm, she said simply, "We never said anything. Just went on to learn what you call stage presence."

She described her life in Hollywood matter-of-factly: she woke up, went to work, came back to her hotel, and went to bed. She tried to defend herself against the columnists who had criticized her life-style: "I walk on the beach and watch the sea. What is that to people?"

Garbo hesitatingly revealed a mystical side to her nature. She was reluctant to talk about it, fearing people would not understand; but she believed in reincarnation and had a strong feeling she had lived before.

She offered opinions on love, marriage, children. She liked children because they were so sensible: "You can say intelligent things to children." Love? That was a woman's "first and last education," and an actress could not portray a woman in love unless she had experienced love herself. As for marriage, she was unsure whether she could spend so much time with one person. She liked to keep her feelings to herself: "Your joys and sorrows — you never can tell them. You cheapen yourself, the inside, when you tell them."

As for her career, she compared it to a love affair. Sometimes the man will hurt the one who loves him, and the woman will try to break off the affair but cannot; she persists in spite of the disappointments. That was how Garbo saw her life as a film actress.

Biery asked her what she would like to do, now that she was rich and famous. Garbo said she wanted to visit China. She had a desire to "touch little things that have been so many thousand years on earth."

Open as she was to Biery's questions, she would not talk further about her family. What were their names? She would not say, for names were not important. She did not think people should talk about each other, for any revelation diminished the feelings that existed between them. She did speak wistfully of Sweden (she had been away from home almost three years). People in America did not realize how Europeans felt when their loved ones left for the United States. They always feared they would never see them again, that they would be swallowed up in the new country. "My people do not realize how short the world is," she said.

At the end of the interview she declared that there was nothing unusual about her life. She was born, she grew up, she had her work, and when it was finished she would travel. That was all, and the private Garbo was never heard from again.

Meanwhile, Stiller was reestablishing himself in Sweden. His first venture was directing a successful musical called *Broadway*. The experience restored his confidence after his Hollywood disaster, but too late. His health was beyond repair, and he entered the hospital in the fall of 1928. He died there on November 8, holding a photograph of Garbo.

Garbo received the news of Stiller's death in a wire handed to her while she was playing a love scene with Nils Asther in *Wild Orchids*. Asther, like Garbo, had been discovered by Stiller. The news of his death affected both of them deeply.

Asther is now retired and lives near Stockholm. He recalled that day in an interview with Sven Broman.

Greta turned deathly white after reading the wire, and for a moment I thought she was going to faint. She walked slowly away from the set like in a trance. The director told us we could take the day off. As I passed Greta's dressing room I heard the sound of laughter. Just then the door flew open and she asked me to come in. "I have something to show you, Nils," she said. She was still trembling, but suddenly she laughed, holding a small perfume bottle in one hand. The tiny bottle was half filled with brandy. Attached to it was a note from Louis B. Mayer, saying, "Dear Greta, my sympathy in your sorrow. But the show must go on!" Mayer told her later of trying to fill the mini-bottle with a teaspoon.

After *Wild Orchids* Garbo told M-G-M again that she needed

77

a holiday and wanted to go to Sweden. This time her request was granted. She left shortly before Christmas 1928.

On the boat from New York to Gothenburg she met the twenty-one-year-old Prince Sigvard of Sweden. The two had occasional meals and drinks together during the crossing, which quickly led to rumors of a romance. But when reporters went to see Garbo at her hotel in Stockholm to ask her about it, she shrugged off their questions, saying, "I don't play around with kids." She was all of twenty-three herself. Still, the prince did play a part in Garbo's romantic life by introducing her in Stockholm to Wilhelm Sörensen, the son of a wealthy Swedish industrialist. Sörensen, a year Garbo's senior, became a frequent escort during her visit, and later followed her back to America.

While in Stockholm Garbo called on Hugo Lindberg, Stiller's executor. She learned to her surprise that her mentor had left a sizable fortune (480,000 kronor, or, then, $95,000), despite the fact that he had had no notable successes — and several failures — in the years before his death. And in his last will, Stiller had bequeathed to "my ever-beloved Greta Garbo" one half of his estate. The other half went to his four brothers in Finland.

Before she left Lindberg's office Garbo said that she wanted to visit Stiller's grave in the Jewish cemetery and asked him for directions. Lindberg offered to take her, but Garbo thanked him and declined, saying, "I would prefer going on my own."

Even on this, her first visit home in three years, Garbo had official duties to perform. She had promised M-G-M's Swedish distributor to help publicize *The Mysterious Lady*. She agreed to pose for two well-known artists in the lobby of the Palladium, where *The Mysterious Lady* would premiere. When she arrived for her modeling assignment, the lobby was a sea of sketchpads. Garbo was furious, and told the M-G-M man, "You told me there would be two artists — I see now you meant two hundred!"

All too soon, the holiday was over; at the beginning of March she was summoned by M-G-M to start work on *The Single Standard*, which was released in July. The tepid reception given the picture proved to the studio that Garbo cast as a nice woman did not sell as well as Garbo cast as one of her detested "bad womens." Her character, Arden Stuart, is tempted by infidelity, but gallantly resists. *The Single Standard* is best remembered today for lovingly photographed moments of an angelic, curly-haired Garbo, and for little else.

On Garbo's return to Hollywood, Harry Edington had decided it was time his client started living more like the star she had become. Her almost tenfold salary increase — for which he was responsible — had done little to change her habits. While other stars had multicourse luncheons served in their studio dressing rooms, Garbo usually made do with a salad or a chicken sandwich prepared by her maid, Alma. Mayer, surprising her once during one of her sparse on-the-set snacks, chided her, "Here we offer you champagne and goose liver, and you don't want it. Why don't you go back to Sweden and eat your herrings and potatoes!" It was only after Edington's pressuring that Garbo, one of the highest paid performers in Hollywood and with ten movie successes behind her, moved from her first modest accommodations at the Miramar to the luxurious Beverly Hills Hotel. Now Edington felt she should have a house of her own, and recommended one on Chevy Chase Drive in Beverly Hills as the most suitable of those he had scouted for her while she was in Sweden. Built in Spanish style, painted white with a red tile roof, it was fully furnished and ready for occupancy. The house was spacious, built in a U-shape with a swimming pool set in the central patio. Most important, it was surrounded by a high wall. Garbo liked it, and agreed to rent it for a year.

Next, with the help of Edington and his wife, actress Barbara Kent, who had appeared with her in *Flesh and the Devil*,

Garbo looked for staff. More than anything she wanted someone able to cook Swedish food and a man to act as chauffeur-
butler. Through the Scandinavian Employment Agency in
Los Angeles she found a young Swedish couple called Gustaf
and Sigrid Norin, who had come to Hollywood some years
before hoping to break into movies, but who had switched to
domestic service as a more secure livelihood. (Gustaf ultimately had some success; he can be seen — briefly — in
Witness for the Prosecution.) They started working for Garbo
in March 1929, helping their new mistress move her few
belongings from the Beverly Hills Hotel to her new home.

Garbo gave her first instruction to Gustaf as she handed
him a gun: "You must never let anyone into the house unless
I tell you to."

Gustaf was put in charge of all buying, but Garbo warned
him that expenditures for food and other household necessaries
were not to exceed seventy-five dollars per month. Gustaf
protested that he would not be able to manage on that and
offered to leave at once. Garbo then raised the amount to a
hundred dollars, and Gustaf promised to try his best. By carefully seeking out the least expensive shops he succeeded in
keeping within the limited budget. Gustaf's duties included
buying all the fan magazines. Rilla Page Palmborg, in *The
Private Life of Greta Garbo*, quotes Gustaf:

She was always anxious to get all the American motion-picture
magazines. Often she would send me down to the drug store for
them days before they were due. . . . Whenever I bought duplicates
of magazines (as I often did, buying so many), she would have me
take them back and get a refund. I also returned many magazines
when it was found that they contained nothing of interest about
Garbo. After Garbo had read all the American magazines she would
have me wrap them up in heavy brown paper and mail them to her
mother. . . . Stamps were Garbo's extravagance. She always put
on nearly twice as many as she needed. She seemed to think that
the more she put on, the faster the letter would go.

In those days Garbo adhered to a strict timetable, rising at seven o'clock when she was due at the studio at nine. The first thing each morning, she went for a swim. On the way to the pool she would look into the kitchen and order a mammoth breakfast of orange or grapefruit juice, chopped beef with fried potatoes and an egg, a piece of cake and coffee — the menu seldom varied. After half an hour swimming laps and jogging around the pool, she would return to her bedroom where she had breakfast sitting up in bed while scanning the morning newspapers for any items of news about her. If she found any she tore them out and stuck them in a scrapbook.

According to Gustaf, Garbo liked dawdling in the mornings and playing with her menagerie of pets — her chow dog, Fimsy, four cats, and a parrot called Polly — all of whom sat on her bed during breakfast. "All of a sudden Garbo would realize that it was nearly nine o'clock. She would hurry her pets out of the room, jump into her clothes, and rush out to the garage. 'Hurry, Gustaf,' she would say, 'drive fast. It makes them mad when I am late at the studio,' " Gustaf recalled. After several unsuccessful attempts, Garbo had given up learning to drive, saying she was too nervous. (Two years earlier, in anticipation of a visit from Saxon, she had written to him consolingly, "You will not need to be driven by me. I have a chauffeur and a new, beautiful Lincoln with a specially built back so that nobody can see the movie ★.")

Nevertheless, these days Garbo was often late arriving at the studio, keeping directors, cameramen, and the rest of the cast waiting while she was made up. She knew she was a star, with power, influence, and an impressive contract, and she often argued with her producers about the merits of her pictures. She usually got her way. Thalberg once admitted, "She really had us all scared around here." Though Mayer grumbled that she was "too highbrow," her integrity was beyond all question. "I would rather have Garbo's word than the signature of many stars I can think of," he said of her.

Garbo also made her own rules about when to quit work. The studio working day normally ran to six o'clock, but Garbo would leave the set on the dot of five, even if it meant breaking off in the middle of a scene. Still, her reputation for being difficult and aloof has been exaggerated. Many who worked with her remembered her as considerate, especially to bit players, whom she helped with their lines; she sometimes joined in the occasional clowning on the set. William Daniels, the cameraman for nineteen of Garbo's Hollywood films, recalled the holiday atmosphere shared by all on the last day of shooting, when Garbo would arrive at the studio laden with gifts for everyone involved. These could range from silk scarves or neckties to silver ashtrays; to Daniels himself she once gave a gold cigarette case.

Arriving home from the studio, she would take a leisurely bath, sometimes for as long as an hour, and read and study her scenes for the next day. Then, unless she expected friends to visit, she would go for a walk before an early dinner. On the Norins' night off, she would prepare her own meal, usually a grilled steak with fried potatoes, which she ate sitting at the kitchen table. Most evenings she was in bed by half past nine, reading a novel or fan magazines.

When Garbo was not working, the routine at Chevy Chase Drive changed. Then she might not get up until noon, or even stay in bed for several days at a time. Sigrid never knew in advance whether her mistress would be in for meals, or, if she went out, how many people she might bring back with her expecting to be fed. If Garbo did order a hot dinner, she might well turn up two or three hours late for it. Sigrid remembers that when Garbo lounged around the garden or the house she always preferred an old bathrobe or bathing suit to any of her elegant negligees. Beautiful clothes seemed to mean nothing to her: Sigrid told Rilla Palmborg, "I never saw her wear any of the evening dresses that hung in her closet. One day she told me she had bought most of those gowns before she went to Sweden. Several of them she never had on, and she was sorry she had bought them." Sigrid never saw Garbo fussing with face lotions or creams. Nor did Garbo like perfume, although friends were always bringing her expensive bottles. The only scent she used was lavender soap.

Plagued by insomnia, Garbo would often stay awake reading until dawn. Today she says her inability to sleep was mostly her own fault either for going to bed too early, or for eating too late when she went to parties.

Gustaf recalled that when Garbo couldn't sleep she seemed to assume that no one else in the house did either: "She was always ringing that bell all through the night. . . . She would call me to put the cats out and bring them in. She would want a glass of water or a certain newspaper. There was always something she wanted in the middle of the night."

The Southern California climate, with its long runs of dry, cloudless days, was uncongenial to Garbo, who missed the cooler — and wetter — Scandinavian weather. When day succeeded day of endless sun, she became uneasy and restless. Then, announcing, "I'll go crazy if it doesn't rain soon," she would put on a bathing suit and go into the garden, turn on the sprinklers, and walk through the spray until she was drenched from top to toe.

Garbo slowly began to make friends, most of them from Hollywood's European community of actors and directors. Through Stiller she had met Emil Jannings, and Jannings introduced her to the Belgian director Jacques Feyder, who directed her in *The Kiss*, and his Parisian wife. Others were Nils Asther, whom she worked with in *Wild Orchids* and *The Single Standard*, and English actor John Loder and his Austrian wife. When together they always spoke German, a language foreign to them all (even, in a sense, to Jannings, who was born in Brooklyn). In this small circle of friends who were professional colleagues she was at her happiest, and she soon was inviting them to Chevy Chase Drive. With them she sat around the fireside talking and joking often late into the night.

But much as Garbo enjoyed their company, there were times when she wanted to see no one. "After a gay time she often lapsed into a moody spell and would stay in her bedroom for days, coming out only to swim or take a walk at night," Gustaf said.

John Loder has recalled,

We often called at her house unexpectedly, just as she called on us. But we didn't always find that her door opened to us. Every so often she would not be at home. Then there would follow days when none of us would hear from her. We couldn't get her on the telephone. No one could find out whether she was working or if she had gone out of town on a vacation. Then all of a sudden she would telephone or appear at the door. She never gave any explanations of where she had been. She went on just as though nothing had happened.

Gustaf said that when one of her spells of refusing to see any of her friends was coming on "she would call me and say, Gustaf, I am not at home to anyone. Remember, not anyone.'" On such occasions Gustaf was known to convey his mistress's instructions literally by saying to the would-be visitor, "Miss Garbo says to say she is not in."

At weekends Garbo liked going to the movies, alone or with a friend, always carefully choosing some out-of-the-way theatre where she was unlikely to be recognized. Often she would see her own pictures two or three times, and she also went to see those of other stars or directors she particularly admired. She never allowed Gustaf to drive the car up to the entrance, but would get out a couple of blocks away. Then, with her hat pulled over her eyes, her coat collar turned up and hands thrust into her pockets, she would hurry inside.

She treasured her solitude, but, contrary to prevailing belief then and now, was no hermit. She loved parties, if the

84

group was congenial. Occasionally, if she was sure she knew all the people present, she delighted the other guests with imitations of other Hollywood stars. She socialized with her friends in the foreign colony, and was seen at the Thalbergs', the Rathbones', the Lubitsches'. She met Salka and Berthold Viertel at a party; the next day, she appeared on the Viertels' doorstep and announced that she had come to continue the conversation of the previous evening. Salka, older and more experienced than Garbo, and with a shared European background — she had been a leading actress in Germany before coming to Hollywood in the late twenties — became a close and devoted friend.

But the mystery around Garbo, as Tallulah Bankhead put it, was as thick as a London fog. Tallulah herself was dying to meet Garbo, and prevailed upon the Viertels to bring about an introduction. In her autobiography, Tallulah remembers that she was so nervous at meeting her idol that she "clowned outrageously," but nonetheless the two stars got on famously together. Later Garbo often went to parties at Tallulah's, where she drank vodka and danced and apparently enjoyed herself immensely.

The fascination of Garbo's "London fog" reached as far as London. In the thirties the much beloved British playwright and actor Ivor Novello visited Hollywood to meet his friend George Cukor, one of Garbo's favorite directors. When Cukor asked if there was anyone in particular he wanted to meet, Novello replied, "Garbo. It's my one and only desire."

Cukor agreed to arrange a meeting, but warned Novello about Garbo's occasional habit of using pseudonyms, among them Harriet Brown, Gussie Berger, Emily Clark, and Miss Swanson. She was at the time in a Harriet Brown phase, and Cukor cautioned Novello to keep up the pretense.

Novello did as he was told and found himself getting on well with "Miss Brown." They met at Cukor's home several times. As their friendship progressed, Novello turned to Garbo casually one evening and said, "Now that we know each other so well, would you mind very much if I call you Harriet?"

No matter what appeared in the press about Garbo's private life, her parties, what she did on her days off, after the 1928 *Photoplay* interview she never offered a word in rebuttal — and certainly did not voluntarily provide material. But when a lucky photographer got a picture of her striding down Hollywood Boulevard dressed in slacks, headlines screamed, "GARBO IN PANTS," and women all over the country raided their husbands' closets.

Garbo had not been at Chevy Chase Drive a year when Gustaf and Sigrid Norin felt they had had their share of adventure in housekeeping for the star, and were ready to quit.

Their decision was triggered by Garbo herself. The star seldom paid attention to housekeeping, but one day she was in a mood when nothing could please her. She called Sigrid to her room to complain about some dust on the floor. Sigrid returned to the kitchen in tears, and she and Gustaf, who still nourished hopes of breaking into pictures, made up their minds to leave as soon as they could. "Garbo wouldn't take us seriously, and two weeks later she had still made no effort to find someone else," said Gustaf. "The night before we were to leave I went to have a talk with her. She was in bed, saying, 'You can't leave me like this. There'll be no one to look after me.'"

Harry Edington, as usual, took on the problem of finding a replacement, and sent Alma, Garbo's personal maid at the studio, to keep house for her in the meantime.

"We said our goodbyes and have not seen Garbo again since," said Gustaf. Looking back on their experience, he said later, "We will never forget the months we lived in the same house with this strange girl. Day after day we saw her without pose or pretense. Yet we never felt that we actually knew her. There was something distant and aloof about Garbo that neither of us could penetrate. She is different from anyone else."

The lease on Garbo's house was due to expire in a few months, and so far she had not been able to find another to her liking. The owner knew that she would not stay on because of neighbors always looking into her garden, and decided to sell the house when Garbo left. There were angry scenes when Garbo refused to let prospective buyers in to look over the property while she was still in residence. When she finally asked for an extension of her lease until she found another place, the irate owner would not grant it, and she had to leave. Garbo's domestic troubles could not have come at a worse time. It was the end of 1929, and M-G-M had decided to put her in her first "talkie."

After the introduction of sound film Garbo had made seven films in which no words were spoken — *Love, The Divine Woman, The Mysterious Lady, A Woman of Affairs, Wild Orchids, The Single Standard*, and *The Kiss*. Although the critics said after *The Kiss* that Garbo was popular enough to attract the public even if she never talked, her producers were eager to have her speak: rumors were beginning to spread that she was avoiding talkies because of her faulty English and an unpleasant speaking voice.

Sound called for an entirely different technique in film-making, imposing new dimensions on acting and speech, and presented the biggest challenge Garbo had to face. Early sound equipment was rudimentary and distorted even a naturally good voice. Rasping and overamplified, the first sound tracks were dreadful. The foreign stars were leaving Hollywood in droves, fearful of revealing inadequate or heavily accented English. German-speaking Emil Jannings was one of many fine actors who left to avoid the risk of sound, and a critic noting his departure asked whether the advent of talking pictures could ever compensate for the loss of "the greatest film actor in the world."

Some observers were not as sympathetic to the very real plight of the European actors in Hollywood. One columnist taunted them in verse:

> Twinkle, twinkle, little star,
> How I wonder what you are,
> French or German, friend or foe,
> Talkie, talkie, then we'll know.

Not many people outside Garbo's immediate circle of friends and professional associates knew that she had an excellent ear. She now spoke American English without the peculiar lilting rhythm many Scandinavians cannot escape. As she had learned to speak flawless German, she now spoke only slightly accented English with a facility few adults could have achieved in five years.

M-G-M worked carefully in putting together Garbo's first sound picture. The script was adapted from Eugene O'Neill's play *Anna Christie*; the fact that both Anna and her father, the play's two central characters, have Swedish accents no doubt influenced the choice. For additional insurance, Charles Bickford and Marie Dressler, both popular and accomplished actors, were also cast. The advance publicity was thunderous. Billboards all across America proclaimed, "GARBO TALKS"; there was no need to explain the reference. The suspense built by studio publicity was continued in the picture itself. Clarence Brown, who directed, does not have Anna appear at all in the first half hour of the film. At last, she enters the waterfront saloon. Silently, slowly, she looks around her, and walks to a table. Finally, she gives her order to the waiter: "Gimme a whiskey with ginger ale on the side. And don't be stingy, ba-bee."

Garbo had talked, and the critics raved. One reviewer described her voice as "rich, full, voluptuous, limpid, incredibly throaty, smoky, sonorous." Another, writing in *Picture Play*, declared it to be "the voice that shook the world."

Meanwhile, the owner of the voice that shook the world was busy with the German-language version of *Anna Christie* (which she enjoyed making, and in which her friend Salka Viertel played Marthy, the Marie Dressler role), and then with filming her second talkie, *Romance*. In the middle of all this she had to look for a new house. In her haste she rented the first one she was shown, taking it on a year's lease at $600 a month. It quickly proved a disastrous move.

The house was situated on Camden Drive, a few blocks from the Beverly Hills Hotel. No one had told her about the nearby streetcar station. The first night in the house she was kept awake by the streetcars, and after a month she was a nervous wreck from lack of sleep. She decided she could stand it no longer, and the search was on again. From that time until the end of her filming days Garbo was to move seven more times, changing homes roughly between every two films.

Wilhelm Sörensen found Garbo her next house. It was near the beach on San Vicente Boulevard. Tall cypress trees lined the long drive to the entrance and the grounds included a lovely garden and velvety lawns. The two-storied, cream-colored stucco house had three bedrooms and two baths.

"I love it all!" she cried. "This will be mine. I'll never move from here as long as I stay in Hollywood."

Garbo was happily installed in her new home when she began work on her next picture, *Inspiration*. Robert Montgomery was her leading man, and Clarence Brown again directed. Then stories made the rounds that Garbo and Brown were having trouble — she called him "old-fashioned" and threatened to walk out and return to Sweden. She swore to herself she would never again work for Clarence Brown (she did, of course, in *Anna Karenina* and *Conquest*). Whatever the sources of friction on *Inspiration*, eventually Garbo decided it was useless to struggle against the odds, and she finished the picture. Covering her lack of enthusiasm for both the film and its director, she shook off her moodiness and was a lively, joking colleague — to the surprise of the others involved in *Inspiration*. But her heart was not in her work. *Inspiration* was not particularly well reviewed. Many critics commented on the disparity between the quality of the script and Garbo's luminous presence. She was playing yet another fallen but ultimately noble woman. But her public stayed with her: over the years Garbo fans forgave their idol murder, adultery, suicide, prostitution, child desertion, and, until the very end, bad scripts.

At home Garbo tried to create her own world. Harry, her Japanese gardener, helped install a comfortable hammock and a table and chairs in the garden; she enjoyed spending time outside with her medicine ball and her dumbbells. She thought she would be free of onlookers, but several times she was surprised by strangers and reacted with a degree of panic unwarranted by the intrusion.

One drawback of the new house was that it lacked a swimming pool. Garbo solved the problem by donning her bathing suit, slipping on a shapeless coat, and going to the beach only five minutes away. No one dreamed that the angular girl wearing a green eyeshade was the idol of millions.

During *Susan Lenox: Her Fall and Rise* in 1931, an assignment she accepted with a sigh of resignation and the comment, "No one can be happy making films," Garbo met a woman who would play an important part in her private life for the next few years.

Mercedes de Acosta was a Spanish-born Hollywood scriptwriter. She was also a vegetarian, a student of oriental philosophies, and a dabbler in esoteric knowledge. Above all, she was a fellow European, and Mercedes and Garbo took to each other immediately. "As we shook hands," Mercedes recalled in her autobiography, *Here Lies the Heart*, "and she smiled at me, I felt that I had known her all my life; in fact, in many previous incarnations." Although Mercedes's cosmopolitan and intellectual background was everything Garbo's was not, each of the women was in her own way a mystic, and their friendship blossomed. It was Mercedes who was sensitive enough to realize that Garbo's mistakes in speaking English often expressed her thoughts better than a precise fluency.

Mercedes involved herself in Garbo's career, making suggestions for roles she should play. She campaigned strenuously in favor of Joan of Arc, and even wrote a script for her friend. Thalberg read it and approved, but Garbo turned it down without comment. At the time Garbo wanted to portray Dorian Gray. Playing a man's role might have been ideal, a *tour de force* — for Garbo, but not for Hollywood. (Mercedes also worked on the screenplay for *Desperate*, for which Thalberg was considering Garbo. She went to Thalberg to discuss her thought that Garbo should wear men's clothes in certain scenes. Thalberg was appalled.)

The exchange of ideas and the support Mercedes offered — and her infectious curiosity about life, which her friend was learning to share — helped keep Garbo from worrying about *Susan Lenox*, which she called "this ghastly film." The story was a true Depression romance. As Susan Garbo played a barefoot farm girl driven by poverty into prostitution. Her plight was received sympathetically by moviegoers, many of whom were themselves on familiar terms with desperation. When the picture was completed, Garbo needed a complete break from Hollywood. Cramped by her work and her professional surroundings, she sought a vacation spot for a holiday with her new friend.

Wallace Beery, who would appear with Garbo in *Grand Hotel*, came up with the ideal answer — a log cabin on a small island in shimmering Silver Lake in the Sierra Nevadas. Solitude was guaranteed.

Garbo and Mercedes were driven to a tiny boat landing by Garbo's chauffeur, James. They loaded their provisions into a rowboat, and with professional strokes Garbo rowed the half mile to the island where the two friends would live in splendid isolation for the next six weeks. Once ashore Garbo's first act was to undress and dive cleanly into the icy black water of Silver Lake.

The vacation, rhapsodically described in *Here Lies the Heart*, was a complete success. Garbo's friendship with Mercedes was confirmed in their idyllic surroundings, as they shared confidences and silences and giggled happily when lumberjacks at the camp where they picked up their fresh milk and eggs took them for schoolgirls. It was with reluctance that they acknowledged to the insistent blasts of the car horn echoing across Silver Lake when James arrived to pick them up six weeks later.

Even as they were driving back through the mountains, the Hollywood machinery was at work preparing another film for Garbo — *Mata Hari*. But before work started, Garbo moved again. This time her choice was influenced by Mercedes, who found the San Vicente Boulevard dwelling "gloomy." She urged Garbo to take a larger house she had found for her on North Rockingham Road. The rent was $1,000 a month, but it had its own tennis court and gardens giving onto canyon and hills. Equally important, it was only a few hundred yards from Mercedes's house.

Garbo took advantage of her tennis court. Although she had never taken a lesson (except from John Gilbert), she was a competent and competitive player. These days she would rise at five in the morning to give herself more time for physical exercise, and when she reported to work on *Mata Hari* she was in excellent condition, lean and tough.

Cast for the second time as a spy, Garbo walks through *Mata Hari* like a countess slumming, curiously detached, until the final unforgettable scene. Then, in black cloak, hair pulled severely back from her face, she appears before the soldiers who will lead her to the firing squad. Her public loved it: *Mata Hari* grossed more than any previous Garbo film.

On the heels of *Mata Hari* came *Grand Hotel*, based on Vicki Baum's novel, in which Garbo worked with John Barrymore. M-G-M spent a fortune on *Grand Hotel*, studded it with stars, and served it up, as one reviewer put it, like a "super-rich pudding." John Mosher wrote in *The New Yorker*, "By her walk alone, her gait, Garbo is exciting, and it doesn't need the folderol of grand dukes and pearls that this story gives her, the so-conventionalized role of the beautiful première danseuse, to lend her that exasperating enchantment vaguely described as 'glamour.' " Again Garbo was seen to shine above what surrounded her.

Shooting of *Grand Hotel* had barely finished when Garbo shared a fate suffered by millions in America and the rest of the world. It was 1932, and the banks were failing. Among those closing was the Beverly Hills First National Bank, at which Garbo kept part of her savings.

More fortunate than most, she had made solid investments in Sweden, which remained unscathed by the crisis. Nevertheless, she was wiped out of ready cash until her next paycheck. Her contract was imminently up for renewal, and Garbo feared that if the hard-nosed M-G-M business heads knew of her predicament, they were quite capable of using it against her to bring down her salary.

At the same time, the lease on the North Rockingham Road house was about to expire. Garbo could not afford to renew, nor could she let M-G-M know that. Mercedes suggested that her friend move into her own house although it meant Mercedes moving out. Garbo accepted the offer, but once installed she peered out the window and called to her friend, "There is no gate. That frightens me. Houses should have gates." That same night Mercedes found a carpenter, persuaded him to break into a lumber yard (leaving a note for the owner), and Garbo had a gate when she awakened the next morning.

Production began on *As You Desire Me*, in which Garbo appeared with Melvyn Douglas and, at her request, Erich von Stroheim. The script was absolutely awful, clumsily adapted from a mystical Pirandello play. There were depths from which not even Garbo could salvage a disastrous screenplay. All three leads seem quite unclear as to what is going on. The picture is memorable for a scene in which Garbo has to play a drunk. Perhaps she drew on dim memories from her hard-drinking homeland, for her performance is no clownish imitation, but truthful and convincing.

After *As You Desire Me*, her contract expired. At loose ends and without a house of her own, Garbo returned to Sweden in the summer of 1932 amid rumors that she had made her last film and would not return. She gave no public explanation for her departure and came under heavy attack by the press, which seemed to have been waiting for this opportunity to voice its grudge against the "Swedish sphinx." One outraged Hollywood journalist wrote:

Greta Garbo left the country without saying goodbye, without even suggesting she was sorry to go. Who is she that she can permit herself such behavior? The world's greatest actress? Well, and what if she is? Sarah Bernhardt was and so was Eleonora Duse, but neither turned her back on the press and public. . . . Crowned heads, millionaires, and famous writers visiting Hollywood have expressed desires to meet Garbo. She has refused. Who is she, we ask, to presume to behave like that? She refused to meet Lady Mountbatten when she visited the studios, refused to meet a royal personage from her own country, refused to have tea with Marlene Dietrich. And to nice, spontaneous Joan Crawford, whose dressing room for many years was next to hers in Metro's star corridor, she has in all that time addressed scarcely a dozen words.

Garbo was being strongly pressured to make a movie in Sweden. It was suggested that she might make a film with a religious theme, possibly about the Salvation Army. The proposal was appealing to Garbo. It brought back memories of her adolescence, when she had performed for the Salvation Army, and of the kindness of John Philipsson, the treasurer of the organization's Swedish branch, who had encouraged her early drive to sing and to act. But M-G-M was not going to let its hottest property be seduced away, especially since her new contract was just being drawn up; negotiated by Edington, it would pay Garbo $300,000 a picture.

During this trip home Garbo renewed her friendship with Max Gumpel, whom she had not seen in ten years; they had met when she was making *From Top to Toe* for PUB. Now a wealthy and successful businessman, he was her companion and tennis partner during her stay in Sweden. But wherever she went she was beset by crowds and reporters, and she soon realized that it was as difficult to maintain privacy in Europe as in Beverly Hills.

Thus, in the spring of 1933, under one of her aliases, she took a freighter back to California via the Panama Canal. She was met on arrival at San Diego by Salka Viertel, who had invited her to stay at her house until Garbo found a new home of her own.

The two had much to talk about. Before Garbo had left for Stockholm, Salka had told Garbo about a biography of Queen Christina of Sweden and suggested Garbo read it and consider portraying the monarch. Garbo was intrigued. She and Salka met with Thalberg, and then Salka and a collaborator prepared a treatment and sent it to Garbo, by then in Sweden. Garbo was delighted, and immediately informed M-G-M that she would sign a new contract if her next picture was *Queen Christina*.

When Garbo returned to Hollywood she brought with her a suitcase full of research material on Queen Christina she had collected in Sweden. She was truly eager to play the brilliant, eccentric seventeenth-century ruler who dressed like a man, negotiated peace for Sweden after years of war, and abdicated at the age of twenty-seven.

Cast opposite Garbo as the Spanish ambassador, her lover, was Laurence Olivier. Garbo had seen his screen tests and had personally chosen him, but when production began it was clear that the combination simply was not working. For several days Garbo tried to overcome her reluctance in playing love scenes with Olivier, but without success. She went to Mayer and requested that John Gilbert replace him. Olivier was told that while he looked the part, he lacked the necessary acting ability.

Rouben Mamoulian was assigned to direct. Garbo admired the attractive, ebullient, and talented Armenian, and worked well with him; soon their friendship was a matter for comment by the press.

Mamoulian is responsible for the remarkable effect of the last scene of the picture. Christina, her kingdom gone, her lover dead, stands motionless on the deck of the ship carrying his body back to Spain. The camera moves toward her until her face, immobile and expressionless, fills the screen for what seems a heartbreaking eternity. Mamoulian shot the scene over and over; his direction to Garbo before the last, and perfect, take, was to think of nothing, to make her mind a blank.

When *Queen Christina* opened in December 1933 it was a tremendous success with the critics, but not at the box office. The American public was escaping the Depression with Shirley Temple, not with Greta Garbo. During 1933 Garbo had ranked fourth in the popularity polls; a year later she was thirty-fourth. There was widespread speculation that her retirement was likely.

Soon after finishing *Queen Christina* Garbo found a suitable house on North Carmelina Avenue in Brentwood. Again,

Flesh and the Devil, 1927

The Divine Woman, 1928

A Woman of Affairs, 1929

The Kiss, 1929

Mata Hari, 1931

Garbo signing U.S. citizenship papers, Los Angeles, February 1951

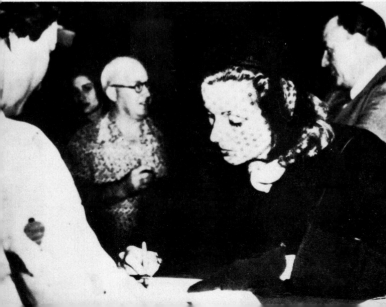

Photograph by Nickolas Muray

Max Gumpel

Garbo on a New York
street corner, 1976

Garbo with Gayelord Hauser

Garbo avoiding
photographers, November 1934

Garbo in *The Single Standard*, 1929

All these photographs of Garbo and Gayelord Hauser were taken by Oliver Woods in the 1940s in Nassau, the Bahamas, and Lake Tahoe, Nevada, and came from a rare album of informal photographs.

An M-G-M still of Garbo sold in Europe as a postcard.

Mercedes de Acosta was her neighbor. With some time available before her next picture, the thought of another joint holiday was irresistible. It was winter, and a Southern California winter was less than appealing to Garbo. Mountains, snow, crisp air — all that Southern California could not offer — beckoned, and Garbo and Mercedes set off for Yosemite.

This trip was not as successful as their first. Garbo traveled as Harriet Brown, one of her preferred names, and Mercedes recalls that Garbo spent — or misspent — a good deal of her time and energy in creating disguises to avoid being recognized. She wore a big lumberjack's cap to conceal her hair. Partly to enhance the disguise, but also because of the cold, she put on layer upon layer of clothing.

Her outfit succeeded too well. There were howls of laughter as she moved like a mushroom across the Yosemite ice-skating rink attracting attention from people who didn't have the slightest idea that this overdressed figure was Greta Garbo. She was unrecognized, but certainly not ignored. Furious, she left the rink.

Still angry, Garbo now insisted on a walk into the wilderness of the sequoia forest, although it was late in the afternoon. She and Mercedes entered the woods as the sun slanted beautifully through the snowy pines. But, faster than they were prepared for, it slipped over a mountain crest and the forest was plunged into near total darkness. A few minutes later they knew they were lost.

For four hours they stumbled, freezing in the darkness as the temperature dropped. Finally Garbo thought she spotted a flicker of light through the undergrowth. They came into a clearing. At a small house an elderly man, quite amazed, let them in and told them that had they continued in the direction they had chosen they would have died before morning. They were walking away from their hotel.

The two women stretched out on the floor and slept until five o'clock in the morning, when the man's son appeared and drove them back in his car. That was enough for Garbo. She returned to Brentwood immediately.

Shooting began on *The Painted Veil*. Once again Garbo found herself in a second-rate melodrama, this one based on a W. Somerset Maugham novel. But as always her approach was serious and complete. Richard Boleslawski, who directed, marveled at her thoroughness of preparation. She always knew her lines and had thought carefully about every scene. Her own suggestions were sound, and she never resented her director's. "She was too good to be true," he said. Boleslawski also noted that she never was guilty of hogging the camera.

Soon after its release in December 1934 it was apparent that *The Painted Veil* would be Garbo's second box-office failure in a row, a record Hollywood's moneymen found hard to swallow. Nevertheless her popular appeal was too great to be ignored so Garbo went on to a more ambitious, literary film, *Anna Karenina*, in which she again worked for Clarence Brown. This time the director sensed Garbo's mysterious appeal and independence and let her act as she saw fit. He even thought she had the makings of another Sarah Bernhardt, "if she would work at her technique. The eyes told it all," Brown said, "her face wouldn't change, but on the screen it would be the transition from love to hate." The critics saw in Garbo's second Anna (her first was in the silent film *Love*) new dimensions, a new tenderness and maturity. Alistair Cooke, reviewing the picture at the time, wrote: "She has suddenly and precisely passed out of her twenties. This quality of gentleness, a gift usually of women over fifty, is an overwhelming thing when it goes with the appearance of a beautiful woman of thirty."

As a deterrent to romantic advances by co-star Fredric March, Garbo munched on garlic before playing love scenes. It worked. March found her to be a healthy, vital girl, and not always as reserved as he had been led to believe. He also noticed her sense of humor.

After *Anna Karenina* Garbo took another long break from work and returned to Stockholm at the end of 1935. Noël Coward was there at the same time, and the two formed a deep attachment. The urbane Coward, no mean hand at bullying when cajolery failed, forced Garbo to go out to theatres, restaurants, and elegant private parties. Frequently Garbo would panic and balk at the last moment. Coward would grab her roughly and shout, "You bloody well *are* going in." And in she would go.

Rumors of romance, hilarious to those who knew them both, helped fuel the insatiable furnaces of publicity. Some reports said an engagement was imminent. The pair had their joke on the press by signing their telegrams and telephone calls with the words "My little bridegroom" and "My little bride." But it was mild revenge for the stories that were published. M-G-M had big plans for Garbo in 1936. She would make her greatest film, which would set her firmly in the footsteps of Duse and Bernhardt. She would make *Camille*.

But on returning to Hollywood Garbo's first task was — once again — to find a house. Mercedes de Acosta had been eyeing one already rented to Jeanette MacDonald. At first the highly popular singer had no intention of moving, but Garbo could find no other house that compared favorably with it and eventually she landed it.

By that time Garbo was deeply involved in *Camille*, for which she prepared as thoroughly as she had for *Queen Christina*. She read everything she could find about Alexandre Dumas's mistress Marie Duplessis, the real-life heroine of his *La Dame aux Camélias*, on which the film was based. Off camera, away from the set, Garbo frequently acted out sequences while apparently enduring intense pain. Strolling on the beach, she would clutch her breast and appear to be out of breath. It is not known if Garbo was really ill at the time; if not, she was nevertheless living out psychologically the role of a tubercular sufferer. Her preparation helped her give perhaps her greatest performance, which reestablished her supremacy. Garbo's Camille has been put under as many critical microscopes as the smile on the face of the Mona Lisa. Years later director George Cukor was quoted as saying, "She was very subtle, able with a slight gesture to be enormously suggestive. In her erotic scenes in *Camille* she never touches but kisses her lover all over the face. Often she is the aggressor in lovemaking. Very original."

Camille was acclaimed by many, but not by all. Don Herold, writing in *The Commonwealth*, spoke bluntly for the dissenters. The release of *Camille* evoked a blast at the Garbo style, which he regarded as "sex on a high horse." Her melancholia was becoming tedious, her face was too severe, and he was tired of watching her throw her head back and laugh knowingly. "It is all too thick, all too, too significant," he wrote. "I say it's spinach."

Camille was followed in 1937 by *Conquest*, a costume drama directed by Clarence Brown that has been described as a $2,800,000 historical distortion. At Garbo's request, Charles Boyer played Napoleon to her Marie Walewska. Norman Zierold in his biography *Garbo* tells two anecdotes about that production. In a scene with Leif Erickson the front of her dress snagged on a button on his uniform and ripped open. Erickson gazed in silent embarrassment; Garbo smiled and said, "I thought it would inspire you." The cameraman on *Conquest* was Karl Freund, who had known Garbo and Stiller years before in Berlin. Once he asked her bluntly what she did about sex. She told him, "Many of the men who ask me out are crazy about my Swedish maid, who is pretty. They pat her on the cheek and flirt with her. But for me at the end of the evening they say, 'Thank you Miss Garbo,' and they tell me how wonderful it was, but not one ever says, 'Let's go to bed.'"

That same year Garbo made another conquest when, through Anita Loos, the Hollywood screenwriter and author of *Gentlemen Prefer Blondes*, she met Leopold Stokowski. She traveled in Europe with him for most of 1938, returning to Hollywood in the fall. Then, in a burst of inspiration on the part of M-G-M, she was cast as Ninotchka.

Ninotchka was a captivating East-West spy-meets-spy comedy. What a discovery! Garbo did not have to die at the end of a movie to ensure its success. But the discovery came too late. Hollywood had waited too long to provide Garbo with a strong new peg on which to hang her future. *Ninotchka* was released in November 1939. War had erupted in Europe, and Hollywood watched its foreign markets disappear. Seven months later Garbo collapsed in tears as she listened to Franklin D. Roosevelt's moving speech condemning Mussolini's cynical entry into the war as France fell. Too upset to comment or be angry, her only words were, "Does anyone have a Kleenex?"

Still, the making of *Ninotchka* had been a happy experience for Garbo. She was in a new house on North Amalfi Drive, near Aldous Huxley and Mercedes de Acosta. Through Mercedes she met Gayelord Hauser, and was entranced both by his natural food diets and his company. She enjoyed working with Ernst Lubitsch, whom she considered one of the great film directors. Advance Hollywood publicity thundered, "GARBO LAUGHS." Perhaps the real meaning was, "GARBO ALLOWED TO LAUGH" — some of her friends wondered whether all the years of sad films had not affected her adversely.

Ninotchka was a triumph, Garbo was superb. But as the war in Europe worsened, her career was ebbing away. Her contract required two more films, and M-G-M sought for a comedy vehicle that would appeal strongly to the American market, since the European outlets, always so lucrative for Garbo films, were lost. In what appears to be sheer madness, M-G-M bobbed Garbo's hair and dressed her to conform with

Hollywood's idea of Modern American Womanhood — not understanding that Garbo's appeal, even to American audiences, lay precisely in her non-American attitudes. She was *not* Mrs. America with a quaint accent, which is what M-G-M reduced her to in the mistaken belief that that was what the public wanted.

The script chosen was *Two-Faced Woman*, a hairy old property that had been resurrected for no good reason and was to prove the *coup de grâce* for Garbo as an actress. When it premiered on December 31, 1941, it met blanket critical and box-office disapproval, and even earned banning by the Roman Catholic Legion of Decency. "It is almost as shocking as seeing your mother drunk," said *Time* in its review. Garbo's reign was over. "I will never act again," she said.

Louis B. Mayer summoned Garbo for a discussion of the situation. Her contract called for one more picture. She listened quietly while Mayer spoke about the difficult times caused by the war. What he really wanted to avoid was throwing good money after bad. Finally, he handed her a check for $250,000 and told her she need not make another film.

There are two endings to this scene: in Clarence Brown's version, Garbo was so insulted that she ripped the check to shreds and stormed out, vowing never to make another picture. In the other ending, Garbo politely handed the check back and said simply, "No, Mr. Mayer. I did not earn it."

The truth? Says Garbo today, "I don't remember!"

RETIREMENT

The Divine GARBO

Chapter 5
RETIREMENT

Two-Faced Woman marked the end of a reign; the goddess left the temple. But the divine Garbo remained inviolate. She never made another movie, never gave another performance, and yet today, nearly forty years later, a chance glimpse of Garbo on a New York street causes the heart to beat faster. Hollywood has never known anyone like her, and since her departure no one has taken her place. Garbo had worked in American movies for sixteen years, making twenty-four pictures. She was only thirty-six years old when she left Hollywood in 1941; her retirement has now lasted for the greater part of her life.

This remarkable retirement was not planned; Garbo intended to return to Hollywood and resume work after the war. She had promised Mayer she would come back if he found a suitable story for her, and M-G-M created a special team whose sole task it was to look for likely properties. Two years later, when Garbo had rejected every one of the scripts sent to her by the studio, Mayer implored Salka Viertel to act as intermediary and bring Garbo to see him to talk about her future. (Salka remembered that after an association of nearly twenty years Mayer still pronounced his star's name "Greeter.") But Garbo felt there was no point to a meeting if there was no story. On her return from a visit to Sweden after the war, in 1946, she told reporters, "I have no plans, either for the movies or anything else. I'm just drifting."

For some years she expected to make a well-timed comeback. Marie Curie, Anna Lucasta, Sarah Bernhardt, George Sand were all suggested as possible roles. But the planning and preparation were never quite right, and to all importunings Garbo had one short answer, summed up in her remark to David Niven: "I had made enough faces." Her own insecurity was a factor; once, years later, she said, "My talents fall within definite limitations. I am not as versatile an actress as some think."

In this postwar period the project that seemed most likely to bring Garbo back was *La Duchesse de Langeais*, based on a Balzac novel. The story and its heroine appealed to her, Max Ophuls would direct, James Mason would play her lover. Contracts were signed, locations in Italy chosen, and she made some costume tests now lost — her only sequences in color. Then in 1950 the enterprise was dropped in a confusion of rumor because of lack of financing.

The failure of *La Duchesse de Langeais* signaled the difficulties of a comeback, and she began to face the fact that she would never make another film. Still, producers all over the world never gave up. Talk of a comeback revived briefly in 1971, with an announcement from Rome that Luchino Visconti had succeeded where a host of others had failed. It was said that he had persuaded Garbo to play the role of Queen Sofia of Naples in *Remembrance of Things Past*, appearing with Laurence Olivier, Marlon Brando, and Alain Delon. Production was to begin in France that summer, but Visconti was unable to raise sufficient money to meet Garbo's demands, and the project was abandoned.

When she left Hollywood Garbo went to New York, where

she lived first at the Ritz Tower Hotel and then at the Hampshire House. After the war she bought a seven-room apartment in a midtown cooperative on East Fifty-second Street, overlooking the East River. This apartment is still her New York home.

In the first years of her retirement Garbo relished her new-found freedom and used it to advantage. Through Gaylord Hauser she met George Schlee and embarked on possibly the most meaningful relationship of her life, which lasted for twenty years. With Schlee she traveled widely and often, and the press called her "The Eternal Vagabond." (Still, she felt some tie to America, and became a citizen in 1951. On that occasion, AP's photo caption reported, "The taciturn Swede, heavily veiled, hurried away without comment.") Summer months were spent with Schlee at his villa, Le Roc, at Cap d'Ail in the south of France. They cruised in the Mediterranean on Sam Spiegel's yacht, *Malahne*, through the Greek islands on Aristotle Onassis's *Christina*. In the spring and fall she hopped between London and Paris, visiting Noël Coward or Cecil Beaton; she counted Princess Margaret among her friends.

Schlee's sudden death in 1964 marked the end of a period of what was, after all, not so hermitic an existence — it had been private and idiosyncratic, but not unsocial. Without Schlee at her side in New York and Europe, she began to withdraw more and more, both in her personal manner and in the circumstances of her life. Her social engagements and friends became fewer, her travels more limited. She turned for comfort to her old friendship with Salka Viertel, from whom she had been separated since her Hollywood days, and spent summers quietly with her in Switzerland.

Today Garbo's New York apartment house, once elegant and still handsome, shows gentle signs of decay through age and lack of repair; there are cracks in the marble-fronted entrance.

On a recent visit the doorman appeared unshaven, his worn uniform in need of pressing. A visitor must be announced by the doorman on a house phone in the lobby. The other tenants have their names and apartment numbers clearly marked on a directory beside the telephone; Garbo's apartment is identified by a solitary G. The elevator stops directly at the door to her apartment. Neighbors and building staff treat her with the respect usually reserved for royalty: they do not speak unless she speaks first, they do not smile unless she smiles first.

Her apartment is a light and airy study in pink. There is no live-in staff, only a cleaning woman who comes in twice a week. Of her seven rooms, four are permanently closed up. The rooms she uses are her bedroom, a large living-cum-dining room, and a smaller room leading off the entrance. One wall of the L-shaped living room has a large fireplace and shelves filled with leatherbound editions of old books; another is hung with paintings from top to bottom. One of these is a valuable Renoir, *Landscape from Antibes*, painted in 1888. Garbo bought the masterpiece at a bargain price of $8,000 at an auction in New York in 1945.

Garbo's daily routine in New York seldom varies. About ten in the morning she puts on a coat and slouch hat pulled over her eyes, dons dark glasses, and wanders through her East Side neighborhood with no destination in mind. "I go out and follow people and go where they're going. I just mill around," she told a friend. The passage of time has not dulled her fear of being recognized, and her outfits, while unobtrusive, have the nature and function of disguises.

Unless she is invited out for lunch she buys food during her morning walk — occasionally indulging in a small tin of caviar — and eats at home alone. After lunch she has an hour's nap, taking the daily papers to bed with her. In the late afternoon she goes out again, looking at shop windows and galleries, but rarely buying anything. Every once in a while she would drop in at the Museum of Modern Art, where she had become friends with Allen Porter of the film department. Occasionally she would ask him to arrange a private showing of one or another of her films. It was to Porter that Garbo imparted the revelation that she had never said, "I want to be alone." She explained to him, "I only said I want to be *let* alone." Their friendship ended abruptly when Garbo discovered that Porter had leaked this sacred morsel of information to the press.

Most evenings Garbo stays at home watching television. At the rare social gatherings she attends these days, she fends off any discussion bordering even remotely on her past career. "It is as if it never existed," one of her friends commented. Garbo's travels are no longer to world capitals and fashionable watering spots, but to a small mountain resort in the Swiss Alps. Here in Klosters she would visit Salka Viertel, the strong and talented woman who had been Garbo's confidante and adviser in Hollywood. She lived in retirement near her writer son, Peter, and his wife, actress Deborah Kerr.

Since the mid-sixties Garbo has spent about two months each summer in Klosters, from the end of July until after her birthday on September 18. Klosters is primarily a ski resort, and is almost deserted at this time of year. The local people ignore Garbo's presence, as if joined in a conspiracy to protect her anonymity.

Garbo's apartment in Klosters is a ten-minute walk from the center of the village, a small first-floor flat in a chalet of four. It is across a short driveway from Mrs. Viertel's house. The back of the chalet overlooks the public tennis courts, where Garbo — at seventy-two — still played an occasional game with a visiting friend. Her life in Klosters is routine. "I rise with the birds and often go to bed while it is still light outside," she told me.

Ordinarily her day begins with a long early morning walk. Then she exercises on her terrace for forty-five minutes before she makes her own breakfast of coffee and toast. About eleven o'clock, dressed in turtleneck sweater, slacks, and walking boots, she takes a leisurely stroll to the village to buy her newspapers and cigarettes. On the way home she stops at the butcher and grocer next door to buy provisions for lunch. Depending on the weather, after lunch she relaxes in a deck chair on the terrace, or has a nap. The afternoon was for visiting Mrs. Viertel.

This was an occasion, for Mrs. Viertel kept open house at tea, and any of her family or friends could drop in unannounced. These could include novelists Gore Vidal and Irwin Shaw and film director Robert Parrish, all of whom maintain homes in Klosters. In this circle Garbo is relaxed and often chatty; she knows and trusts these friends, who make no demands on her. "Shaw is Garbo's favorite amid the mob," one of them told me. Ever jovial, Shaw occasionally takes Garbo out for dinner, either to his own apartment or across the street to the smart Chesa Grischuna hotel, whose proprietor, Hans Guler, is also a friend and protector. Journalists who have gone to Klosters in the hope of catching Garbo on these summer vacations and have tried to extract information about her from any of her friends are given short shrift; and Herr Guler never fails to alert Garbo if a newsman or photographer has checked into one of his hotels. Garbo then stays home, waiting for Guler to tell her that the enemy has departed.

"I'm just drifting," Garbo said in 1946. And so she has — for thirty years. Her accomplishments during her long retirement have been equal to nil. Her abnormal life-style, apparently devoid of all interests and devoted to the pursuit of killing time, produced in her an ever-growing void that made her discontented and egocentric. She seems to think little about anything but what is concerned with herself. By giving nothing she has received little in return.

And yet when she was giving — making picture after picture — she received little that truly meant anything to her.

109

She played Camille and Ninotchka, yes — but she also spent much of her career portraying what she called "bad womens" in movies she thought little of. She had come to Hollywood a star at the age of nineteen and plunged into an unfamiliar and uncongenial world whose language she did not speak. Her second picture was the occasion of the disgrace and banishment of Mauritz Stiller, possibly the one artist who could have helped her become the performer she wished to be.

Garbo was shy, inexperienced, and intelligent. She learned quickly that only by withdrawing could she exert any control whatever over the use others would make of her talent. "I've got so much," she wrote to Saxon, "and still I'm boundlessly ungrateful."

Chapter 6
MEN

The Divine GARBO

Chapter 6
MEN

Garbo never married. In 1928, when not quite twenty-three years old, she wrote from Hollywood to her friend Lars Saxon: "I think about the time when I will be able to settle down in peace at home. Then, Lasse, we will have our bachelor evenings and drinks because I will probably remain a bachelor. I cannot see myself as a wife — ugly word."

But there were men.

Of all the men in Garbo's life none has played a more decisive part or left a more lasting imprint than Mauritz Stiller. To him she owed her greatness as a star. A striking looking man, tall, thin, and rugged-faced, with a crop of thick hair and bushy eyebrows, his talent was brilliant and his manner theatrical. He was a leading director in Swedish film at thirty-eight when Greta Gustafsson, not yet fifteen but aflame with determination to become an actress, sought him out in the spring of 1920. Three years later she appeared in Stiller's production of *The Saga of Gösta Berling*, and in late June 1925 the two sailed for New York on the first stage of her ultimate triumph — and his downfall.

Demoralized when Hollywood failed to appreciate or understand his art and techniques, Stiller returned to Sweden in 1927, leaving his protégée in Hollywood. When he died, on November 8, 1928, he was only forty-five.

Garbo worshiped Stiller. He had taught her everything she knew, from how to turn her head to how to express love — and hate. She followed his every whim, wish, and demand. She lived her life according to his plans. He told her what to say and what to do, and she obeyed.

The true nature of their relationship has been the subject of much conjecture and speculation. Even Stiller's closest friends, both in Stockholm and Hollywood, who could be expected to know the truth, vary in their opinions.

Lars Hanson, the Swedish actor who starred with Garbo in Stiller's production of *The Saga of Gösta Berling* in 1923 and was an old friend of the director, said: "I saw them always together but I could not see that Stiller had a personal interest in Garbo except a strictly professional one. And there it ended."

Victor Sjöström, the Swedish film director who was already working in Hollywood when Stiller and Garbo arrived, saw it differently. He said: "For a certain time at least Stiller was in love with Garbo, and she with him. They told me so themselves."

Nils Asther, the Swedish actor and friend of the couple, lends support to Sjöström's appraisal. He was in Hollywood filming *Wild Orchids* with Garbo when the cable with the news of Stiller's death was handed to her on the set. "She stood there with her face hidden in her hands, not able to believe it could be true," Asther said. "A few days later Garbo left Hollywood secretly for New York and checked in under another name at the Hotel Commodore, where she and Stiller had spent their first few months when they arrived in America. She could not be with him ever again, she said, so at least she wanted to relive the memory of him. Yes, she loved him very much, though I don't think that sex played any part in it."

It is likely it didn't. Like several of Garbo's men, Stiller was a homosexual.

When Stiller died, Garbo found herself a ship without a rudder. She was bewildered, lost, and very lonely. For several years she continued to speak of him as if he were alive, referring to him by his pet name, Moje. Friends never ceased to be touched by her lasting devotion to him, and indeed she had once said, "If I were ever to love anyone, it would be Mauritz Stiller."

At the end of 1928, a tired Garbo — she had made eight films in three years — returned on her first visit to Sweden. There she learned that Stiller's home and furniture were to be sold by auction. She attended the sale and when the estate manager showed her around she touched many of the objects, remembering their origins and associations. She bought an off-white, seventeenth-century Scandinavian table that today stands in the living room of her New York apartment.

When Garbo left for Hollywood with Stiller in 1925, the move was against the wishes and advice of a young Swede named Lars Saxon.

Born in 1900, Saxon was the son of a Stockholm publisher. At seventeen he joined the family firm, Saxon and Lindström, and six years later, in 1923, he became the first editor of *Lektyr*, a weekly magazine still published today. At about this time, through Vera Schmiterlöw, he met Garbo, who was filming *The Saga of Gösta Berling*.

"Lars was really in love with Greta," according to Harry Leksén, one of Saxon's best friends in those days. Now a retired businessman in his eighties, he told Sven Broman:

Lars was one of the first in our gang to have a car. In fact, Lars had his first car when he was fourteen years old. When he met Garbo he had a big Packard. Lars was an early bird. He lived rather close to me in a suburb of Stockholm. I had no car at the time, and Lars would pick me up early in the morning and take me to my job in the city. After that he would drive downtown to pick up Greta and take her to the studio, to the Academy, or anyplace else she needed to go. Lars talked about Greta a lot, but I never did meet her.

But Saxon's passion was not returned. She liked Lars, who was handsome, well mannered, who always cared about her. But she looked on him as no more than a good friend. Not surprisingly, then, he was unable to dissuade Garbo from going to America with Stiller.

She left Sweden. And it was then, at long distance, that her relationship with Saxon became vitally important to her.

Garbo's correspondence with Lars Saxon during her first three years in America sustained and comforted her. Written in a large, strong hand, usually in pencil, on the stationery of hotels and the M-G-M studios, her letters to him over those years were long and frequent.

Lars Saxon was a faithful friend. He came to visit Garbo in Hollywood in 1927, telling his family that he would be studying the American press; he was one of the first to welcome her when she returned to Sweden on her first visit home, in 1928, meeting her on the train to Stockholm. Still, by now it was clear that there was no romantic future for the pair. Greta returned to America, Lars married and pursued a successful career in Sweden as a publisher and author. A diabetic, he died in 1950 at the age of forty-nine.

Incidentally, Lars Saxon was responsible for Garbo's only published work: in 1927 and in 1931, two series of articles appeared over her name in his magazine, *Lektyr*.

The noisiest of Garbo's several much-publicized Hollywood romances was her legendary affair with her leading man, John Gilbert, who was billed as "the screen's perfect lover." The blonde, twenty-one-year-old Garbo and the handsome, twenty-nine-year-old Gilbert — raven-haired, with blazing eyes

115

and gorgeous teeth — met on the set of *Flesh and the Devil* in 1926. Before Garbo appeared on the scene he had been twice married and twice divorced.

Gilbert was the hottest property among the male stars of the silent screen, earning $10,000 a week; he was more highly paid than Rudolph Valentino. Described as tempestuous, highly strung, reckless, Gilbert was considered by M-G-M the ideal quarry for the cool, reserved Swedish recluse. In pairing them there could be no doubt of success. All that was needed was a love story sufficiently intense. *Flesh and the Devil*, in which Garbo would play a passionate, unfaithful wife and Gilbert her lover, was considered the ideal choice. It was.

The stars were perfectly matched. The daring love scenes in *Flesh and the Devil*, superbly photographed by William Daniels, are almost voracious — and totally convincing. To add stimulus to their screen romance and whet the public's appetite, M-G-M issued regular bulletins on the progress of the love affair. Clarence Brown, the film's director, pronounced: "I am getting the best love scenes ever because I'm working with raw material. They are in that blissful state of love that is so like a rosy cloud that they imagine themselves hidden behind it, as well as lost in it."

Hyperbole and the needs of publicity aside, the relationship was real. During filming of *Flesh and the Devil* Garbo and Gilbert became increasingly "good friends," and she often visited his home in Beverly Hills. He nicknamed her "Fleka," a slight variation of the Swedish word "flicka," meaning "girl." She called him "Jacky" — pronounced, of course with an initial "Y." Together they would go for long drives and picnics in the mountains, or relax at Gilbert's house, playing tennis or swimming. There is no doubt that he loved her.

In the course of the two years they worked together, Gilbert repeatedly asked Garbo to marry him, but she refused each time, saying that she did not want to discuss it. She wrote to Saxon: "I suppose that you have read in the newspapers about me and a certain actor, but I am not 'going to be married.' They are wild for news, so they fell upon me." Publicity and gossip surrounded their every move, and frightened her.

Still, more than once Gilbert actually believed they would marry. On one occasion a wedding was set and a honeymoon planned for the South Pacific aboard a yacht which Gilbert had romantically outfitted especially for the occasion and named the *Temptress*. But when the crucial moment approached, Garbo took to her heels. Later her courage returned, and she seemed ready to elope with him. The couple drove to Santa Ana, where they headed straight for the marriage license bureau. But Garbo once more shied at the last moment and ran away, locking herself in the ladies' room of a nearby hotel. After this incident Gilbert gave up trying.

When asked to comment on their on-and-off romance and the chances of marriage, an irate Gilbert told a reporter:

She says she'll marry if I let her retire from the screen. She hates acting. She hates Hollywood and everything in it. She wants to buy half of Montana or whatever state has no people in it and turn it into a wheat farm and raise wheat and children. She keeps saying, "You're in love with Garbo the actress." And you know, I say, "You're damn right." Frankly, I don't want to marry some dumb Swede and raise wheat and have kids miles from civilization.

Somewhat more calmly, on another occasion Gilbert complained that Garbo was always "holding back something — guarding a part of herself, even in romance." It was hard to take, he said.

The end of their liaison coincided with the last of a series of three films they made together, A *Woman of Affairs*, released in 1929. Once the fabled love affair was over, Gilbert quickly sought solace elsewhere. The same year he married another well-known actress, Ina Claire. Reporting their sudden wedding, one newspaper headed its story: "GARBO COLLAPSES AS GILBERT MARRIES." Shortly afterward Garbo told a friend, "There never was a romance between us. I wonder what I ever saw in him. I guess he was pretty."

Four years later Garbo made one more film with Gilbert, *Queen Christina*, after having rejected one by one all other leading men who had been proposed for the role. But Gilbert's reputation was sinking fast, and his performance in *Queen Christina* did not redeem it.

In the interval Gilbert's marriage to Ina Claire had ended and he married his fourth wife, Virginia Bruce. After *Queen Christina* he made one more film, but his slide into obscurity was almost complete. His fourth marriage a failure, his fortune gone, Gilbert was thirty-eight when he died of a heart attack in 1936.

The Garbo–Gilbert affair was finally over when Garbo sailed from New York on her first visit back to Sweden in December 1928. An acclaimed star, she had three years of Hollywood behind her. She was only twenty-three.

On the voyage she met the twenty-one-year-old Prince Sigvard, a son of the late king of Sweden, and found him amusing. Garbo suggested that they should plan a party on New Year's Eve at her hotel in Stockholm. Among those the prince brought along to the celebration at the Strand Hotel was the tall, blond Wilhelm Sörensen, a twenty-four-year-old law student and son of a wealthy Swedish industrialist.

The next day Sörensen sent Garbo a box of chocolates and with it a book by one of Sweden's best-loved poets, Harriet Löwenhielm. One of the poems, written in English, became a Garbo favorite:

May we be happy and rejoice
on this green earth, oh, my son
but tired and smiling
we leave our toys
when it's over and life is done.

When Sörensen telephoned Garbo at her hotel shortly afterward to ask if he could see her again, he received an evasive
reply. "Should I know?" said Garbo, "I'll call you back." A
baffled Sörensen was left holding the phone. In later years,
"Should I know?" became a Garbo byword that confounded
even her best friends.

During her three months' stay in Sweden, Garbo and
Sörensen saw each other frequently, taking long walks, visiting
the theater, dining with friends. Once they were invited by
one of Sörensen's aunts, the Countess Hörke Wachtmeister,
to stay at her castle south of Stockholm. At first Garbo was
reluctant to go, fearing a crowd of fashionable and curious
guests. On being told that she and Sörensen would be the
only guests she accepted the invitation, exclaiming, "Oh, how
exciting. It will be the first time I stay at a real castle!" But
soon after arriving, Garbo received a message instructing her
to return to Hollywood without delay, to begin production of
The Single Standard.

Garbo and Sörensen arranged to spend their last evening
in Stockholm, having dinner at the fashionable Cecil, where
black tie for men and long dresses for women were a rule of
the house. Earlier in the day Garbo had visited her mother
to say goodbye, then gone to her hotel to pack. She had had
no time to change before dinner, and arrived at the restaurant
still in the sports dress and heavy snow boots she had worn
all day.

Sörensen had chosen a discreet corner table, and at first no
one paid attention to Garbo's attire. But later in the evening
Garbo said she wanted to dance. The couple had hardly

reached the small dance floor when an embarrassed manager, pointing to Garbo's boots, asked them to return to their table.

Garbo asked "Sören," as she called him, to accompany her to Gothenburg the following day, where she was to board the *Gripsholm* for New York. News of her departure had spread quickly, and there were crowds at the dock. Finally alone with Sörensen in her cabin, Garbo threw her arms around him and told him, "Sören, come to America and join me. Soon, very soon."

A few months and many family quarrels later Sörensen gave up his law studies and followed Garbo to the United States. The journey took fifty-six days on a cargo ship.

Sörensen described his friendship with Garbo in long talks with Sven Broman in the fifties.

Her words rang in my ears after she left Gothenburg: "Sören, come to America and join me." Two days later I had a cable with the same words. And the week after, three more. Finally, from the train to Hollywood, just one word: "Come."

When I broached the subject to my father, he was furious and adamant in refusing me permission to go. But I persisted daily until he finally gave in, saying it was perhaps as good studying movies in Hollywood as law in Sweden.

Instantly I wrote to Garbo, letting her know I would be coming shortly. Her answer was less enthusiastic than I expected. "If you really wish to come," she wrote, "you are heartily welcome, but I must warn you that you may never understand me completely — *how* I really am, and *what* makes me so. If I am working on a movie when you are here, we would not see much of each other, because then I must be alone."

There was also a pessimistic note about her letter when she added, "They are making sound movies here now, and nobody knows what is to happen to me. Perhaps I will not stay here much longer. Already some of the top stars intend leaving Hollywood, and it is questionable for how long I can remain a film tramp."

I did not let her letter put me off, and I left soon afterward, taking a cargo ship belonging to one of my father's business friends going to San Pedro, California, via South America. The voyage took two months.

Some days before arriving I cabled Garbo asking if she would like to meet me and have lunch on board ship before disembarking. She answered, "Will come if not too many people."

The ship pulled into port in the early morning. Looking through the porthole of my cabin I suddenly saw Garbo walking up the gangway in quick strides. When she saw me she said reproachfully, "You seem in no special hurry. I thought you would come running to me, but such is my life, always to be disappointed."

We stayed for lunch on board ship, with the captain and officers joining us, and everyone drinking to each other's health.

Garbo had invited me to stay at her home at Chevy Chase Drive until I found a place of my own. The first thing I saw on entering the house was a vicious-looking chow with red fur and red eyes, ready to pounce on me if I came any closer. Noticing my fear, Garbo said, "He's very old and has almost no teeth." Then she pointed to the house and said, "This is a very crazy place. It has rooms in all directions. I have prepared a guest room for you upstairs on the left; my room is far away at the other end."

We had coffee on the patio beside the swimming pool, and Garbo told me that we were invited to visit Ernst Lubitsch for cocktails later in the day. There were already a lot of people there when we arrived, and as Garbo entered, there was a sudden hush. Judging from the look of surprise on everyone's face, it was obvious that she was seldom seen attending parties.

Garbo introduced me to Jacques Feyder, another top director at M-G-M. He later gave me a job as his assistant. I was disappointed when Garbo turned down Lubitsch's invitation to stay on for dinner, but she said that she wanted to have dinner with me alone at home to hear about her mother and brother and all the latest gossip from Stockholm. That same evening she told me about her plans to go away for a short holiday in the north of California.

Garbo had a Swedish couple, Gustaf and Sigrid Norin, working for her. Next morning Gustaf drove me to Hollywood to help me find a room at a hotel. When Garbo left I felt very lonely. To my delight she called me after a few days, saying she did not like it where she had gone, as there were too many people. My heart jumped with joy when she announced her intention to return the following day.

Around this time was the transition to "talkies" and all Hollywood was anxious, Garbo and the top people at M-G-M no less than anyone else. Her silent films were still breaking box-office records, but no one knew how well she would do in the changeover to sound.

Many times she asked me home to rehearse her *Anna Christie* lines with her by reading opposite parts. I was amazed at how easily she learned and her good memory. If I ventured once in a while to add some dramatic touch to my part in reading, she would quickly pull me down to earth, saying. "Don't fiddle-faddle, just read it straight!"

One day she called me excitedly, saying, "Tomorrow, Sören, tomorrow it happens. Tomorrow I shall start talking in the movie." She asked me to come to dinner that night and afterwards go for a long walk with her in the hills.

When Garbo works she rises at five A.M. — if she can sleep at all. When I left her that night she said she would call me in the morning. But she called at half past two, and asked me to come at once. We sat around drinking coffee and talking until six. Then she asked me to come with her to the studio. It was the first time. It was still dark and foggy when we left her house. She put a rug around her in the car and for a while we drove in silence. Suddenly she said, "Sören, I'm an unborn baby now."

Alma, her maid, and Billy, her hairdresser, were already waiting when we reached her dressing room. They loved Garbo, but I sensed they were on edge. Turning to me, Garbo said, "Now you can go, Sören, but please stay in the studio. We can have lunch together later."

I whiled away the time in Jacques Feyder's office until just before noon, when Garbo sent a message for me to come to her dressing room.

She was a changed person, almost unrecognizable from the Garbo I had left a few hours before. Not the "unborn baby" of that morning, but a gay young woman full of self-confidence and free of worry. "It was not as bad as I feared, but I was still scared when I heard my own voice," Garbo said. The first line she had to speak was: "Gimme a whiskey! Ginger ale on the side!"

I had heard her say these words over and over again during our home rehearsals. Now all in the studio were holding their breath, waiting to hear them again during the playback. Alma was almost out of her mind with worry, and prayed to the Lord. Billy wept hysterically, and even hardened technicians were visibly affected. Then Clarence Brown, the director, came over and kissed her, and said, "Fine, Greta, really fine."

Garbo's voice was a sensation. M-G-M knew that they had struck it rich. They also decided to maintain a total blackout on news during production. This sparked off rumors that something had gone wrong with Garbo's first talking picture.

As soon as the movie was finished Garbo wanted to get away for a rest, and she asked me to come with her. Shortly afterward large ads started appearing in the newspapers: "GARBO TALKS." Meanwhile M-G-M was making arrangements for a super première. They wanted Garbo to attend, but Garbo said no. Instead, we went a day later, slipping into the theatre unnoticed. We left just before the end and I could see that Garbo was satisfied, even if she was mildly critical of parts, saying she could have done better.

The reviews of *Anna Christie* were unanimously outstanding. One critic raved, "The voice that shook the world!"

Some time afterward, while relaxing by her swimming pool, Garbo said quite unexpectedly, "Sören, if you had enough money, where would you like to live?" I answered that I had never given it a thought, but maybe on the French Riviera. Looking puzzled, she continued, "Tell me, on which island is Nice situated?" I pointed out that Nice is not on any island, but on the southern coast of France. "We will not discuss it further," said Garbo. "I studied geography at school, you know."

One day before I left Hollywood for good, Garbo told me that she wanted to change her account from one bank to another. A great part of her money was then in bonds and shares. She asked me to go with her to her new bank, where she had to cut some dividend coupons off bonds she kept in her safe deposit box. But she had no scissors, and sent me to get a pair. I came back and handed them to her. She told me straight out, "Go and wait for me outside. You don't have to see how much money I have." So like her — ever secretive about everything.

His Hollywood apprenticeship served, Sörensen returned to Sweden to take a job with RKO in Stockholm. After nearly two years at Garbo's side as friend, confidant, helper, his departure caused no stir.

When Sven Broman asked Sörensen whether he thought Garbo was a happy person, he replied, "It's hard to say. I don't think Garbo herself knows the answer. She has paid a very high price for the life she leads."

Sörensen did not see Garbo again until she visited Sweden with Leopold Stokowski in 1938. While in Stockholm she called Sörensen to ask if he could arrange a private showing of her first feature film, *The Saga of Gösta Berling*. "It was the movie I loved most of all," she told him.

"But when it was over," Sörensen recalled, "Garbo was downcast and sad. She insisted on taking the elevator alone down to the street. I never saw her again after that."

Wilhelm Sörensen suffered from ill-health during the last years of his life, and died in his early sixties. Like others of Garbo's closest friends — before and after him — Sörensen was a homosexual.

The nearest Garbo ever came to marriage was her engagement — if such it was — to Max Gumpel in 1932.

Garbo had known Gumpel since she was a teenager. They met at PUB during the filming of *From Top to Toe*. The little boy in the cast was Gumpel's nephew, and when Uncle Max visited the set he was immediately taken with Garbo. Although fifteen years older than she, he soon became her "sweetheart." They went out together often, then drifted apart when Garbo entered the Royal Dramatic Academy in 1922. In the following ten years, as Garbo rose to fame and stardom, Gumpel became a millionaire construction engineer.

When Garbo arrived in Sweden for a long visit in 1932, she telephoned Gumpel. At first he thought the call was a hoax. Once he was sure that it was really Garbo, he invited her for dinner. They were often seen together during her stay, and there were soon rumors of a new romance.

Vera Schmiterlöw recently told Sven Broman in Stockholm: "Max was Greta's first big love. We saw one another when she came back and one day she called me to say that she and Max had become engaged and he had given her a ring. Greta told me that she was very happy about it, but I don't believe that she took it very seriously because all the time she talked about it she was laughing and seemed to treat it like a big joke."

Another who remembered the engagement is a Swedish-American businessman, Eric Ericson, a friend of Gumpel's for many years. Ericson told Broman about being invited by Gumpel to lunch with him at the Grand Hotel in Stockholm.

Max arrived at the hotel with Garbo arm-in-arm. He hadn't said anything about bringing her before. When the meal was over they announced to me their decision of becoming engaged, right then and there. With that, Max took a diamond ring from his coat pocket and slipped it on Greta's finger, saying to me, "So now we are engaged, and you are our witness, but don't tell anyone about it." I left soon afterward for the United States, and heard no more.

No one heard any more. Gumpel died in 1965 at the age of seventy-five. He had married twice and fathered six children.

By the spring of 1933 Garbo had had enough of Europe and was glad to return to California to prepare for her next film, *Queen Christina*.

Sailing under an assumed name on a Swedish freighter, she hoped to disembark unnoticed. The only person she told of her return and asked to meet her on arrival at San Diego was Salka Viertel, co-author of the *Queen Christina* screenplay.

But awaiting an unsuspecting Garbo on the pier as she stepped off the boat was a large gathering of reporters wanting to know about reports of her engagement in Sweden to Max Gumpel. "Are you in love? When are you getting married?" They fired the questions at her. Garbo's only reply was, "No comment."

The reporters were soon able to ask her about a new romance — with her director in *Queen Christina*. Rouben Mamoulian was a tall black-haired Armenian with melancholy eyes. At thirty-five, he already had established a successful stage career as a Broadway director. M-G-M had chosen him to direct *Queen Christina* because of his reputation for technical innovation in early sound films.

Garbo was instantly impressed by Mamoulian's personality. She also responded well to his excellent direction. Before long the two were seen together out on the town. During a shooting break of several days the couple set off on a trip to the Grand Canyon, pursued by the press, who suspected them of eloping.

There was no elopement. Indeed, if there ever was any real romance at all, it was over by the time *Queen Christina* was completed at the end of the year.

A close woman friend of Garbo's has told me, "She did not want to be captured, either mentally or in bed, and resolutely evaded all attempts." Until now, capture by any of the men romantically linked with Garbo hardly seemed imminent. Then she met a man who was as strong a star as she was.

Garbo was thirty-two when she met Leopold Stokowski, internationally renowned conductor of the Philadelphia Orchestra from 1914 to 1936. "I felt the electricity going through me from head to toe," Garbo told her friend.

They were introduced, at Stokowski's request, by Anita Loos in Hollywood in 1937. The maestro's charm was irresistible, and Garbo was untroubled by the twenty-three-year difference in their ages. A few months later, Garbo had finished *Conquest* and Stokowski's second wife was obtaining a divorce. Nothing opposed a holiday; and soon the pair were in Europe.

Stokowski had rented the Villa Cimbrone in Ravello, Italy, from an American friend and traveled ahead alone. He was joined by Garbo a few days later on her return from a visit to her family in Sweden. For a few days they could enjoy walking through the village arm in arm, but their identity soon became known and the press lay siege to the Villa Cimbrone. Four policemen with dogs were stationed at the entrance to keep invaders at bay. For the next three weeks the couple lived like prisoners, unable to set foot outside the grounds.

Stokowski, a health fanatic, was observed walking in the garden and initiating Garbo in the art of yoga. Reporters watched them exercise together each day. Desperate for copy, the newsmen considered no story too absurd to report. They quoted a waiter at the Hotel Caruso, where Garbo and Stokowski had been fond of taking a vegetarian repast when it was still safe to do so, who commented that the gentleman must really be in love, for before the beautiful lady came Stokowski used to order heaping plates of veal, sausage, and pasta. Another dispatch solemnly described how Garbo milked a cow while Stokowski stroked the animal's head.

At the end of three weeks Garbo agreed to receive the press on the understanding that they would then go away and leave the couple alone.

When asked whether she and Stokowski intended to get married, Garbo shook her head. Then she said:

There are some who want to get married and others who don't. I have never had an impulse to go to the altar. I haven't many friends and I haven't seen much of the world. My friend, Mr. Stokowski, who has been very much to me, offered to take me around and see some of the beautiful things. I optimistically accepted. I was naïve enough to think I could travel without being discovered and without being hunted. Why can't we avoid being followed and examined? It is cruel to bother people who want to be left in peace. This kills beauty for me.

When one reporter asked her specifically if she had plans for marriage any time in the future, Garbo replied, "I wouldn't know. There seems to be a law that governs all our actions, so I never make plans." She stood up. The interview was over.

A few days later the couple left Ravello on a motoring trip across Europe, ending with a visit to Sweden in May. There they stayed for three months on a country estate called Hårby, south of Stockholm on Lake Sillen, which Garbo had bought some two years before. Behind large signs reading "ABSOLUTELY PRIVATE," Garbo and Stokowski at last found the privacy both sought. They were able to go out in pursuit of their pleasures unmolested, marketing in the nearby village and visiting friends. For Garbo this was the life she had been longing for.

No one had seen her look happier or more radiant. She called Stokowski "Stoky" and referred to him as "my boyfriend." Friends thought them an ideal couple.

But not long afterward the "honeymoon" was over, ending as suddenly as it had begun only ten months before. Stokowski returned to the United States alone. Two months later Garbo arrived back in New York and granted a surprise shipboard interview to the waiting press. Asked whether she and Stokowski were already married, Garbo answered curtly, "You would know all about it if we were."

Did she think she would ever marry? "If I could find the right person to share my life with, perhaps I would."

During the few days she spent in New York before leaving for Hollywood Garbo and Stokowski did not see each other.

They never met again.

Several years later, Stokowski tried his hand at marriage once more. On a visit to Nevada he met Gloria Vanderbilt as she was getting a Reno divorce from her first husband, and married her on the spot. For the aged Stokowski it was to prove his third marriage failure. Fifteen years after their divorce, Stokowski died in England, the country of his birth. He was ninety-five.

Leopold Stokowski had introduced Garbo to yoga. He also led her to Gayelord Hauser. She became the most famous disciple of the handsome and personable German-American dietician and author of *Look Younger, Live Longer*.

As Hauser recalls in his book *Treasury of Secrets*, he received a telephone call in Hollywood from Garbo one day, asking if she could come to see him.

She arrived — a vision of breath-taking beauty, with her long hair and fresh golden complexion.

Miss Garbo had heard of me through her friend Leopold Stokowski, and she came to see me because of her great interest in food. She was at that time following a diet consisting mainly of boiled vegetables and thou-shalt-nots.

In spite of her radiant beauty, this diet had had a marked effect on her vitality; she was suffering from overtiredness and insomnia, and was in danger of serious anemia.

I made it my task to wean her away from strict vegetarianism, and coax her back to intelligent eating — no easy chore with a woman who has a will of steel. Finally she consented to try my suggestions. First of all, of course, I insisted on a balanced diet. The next day, when I stopped by her dressing room at lunchtime, I found that she was having her usual vegetables, in her usual privacy — but this time the vegetables were raw, in a large salad bowl, and well fortified with protein: bits of ham, chicken, cottage cheese, and wheat germ. She had begun the high-vitality program, and she quickly regained her energy.

Soon after Miss Garbo began this new way of nutrition, she accepted the leading role in the film *Ninotchka*, widely publicized with the wondrous statement, "Garbo Laughs!" Many people congratulated us both on the "new" Garbo.

Garbo, then thirty-three, was enchanted with the dashing dietician. Ten years older than she, charming and well connected, Hauser became her frequent escort. He even had the improbable idea of making her his wife. Soon after the première of *Ninotchka* Garbo and Hauser left together for a vacation in Florida. The newspapers had a field day again, speculating on a coming marriage. The couple were, Louella Parsons declared, "thataway."

Hauser had given Garbo a diamond ring before they left on the trip. While in New York, the far from publicity-shy Hauser secretly supplied a news bureau friend with an advance story of his coming wedding to Garbo, promising to confirm their marriage after the ceremony had been performed.

The holiday lasted a month, but no wedding took place. Then the affair cooled, although Hauser continued to be Garbo's close friend for many years. Ironically it was Hauser who introduced Garbo to George Schlee, a Russian-born New York millionaire. He was to become the next — and the longest lasting — of Garbo's men.

When Garbo complained one day to her friend Gayelord Hauser of having "nothing to wear," he took her to Valentina to buy new clothes. The famous star soon became friends with the famous designer, and the friendship soon included the designer's husband, George Schlee.

Garbo was forty and still regarded as the world's most beautiful woman when she met Schlee. Their relationship became the most meaningful of any in her life and lasted for close to twenty years, until his death.

Schlee was a man of the world, a millionaire and business

partner of his wife, Valentina. The three were seen often together until, in time, it was Garbo and Schlee alone. Speculation reached its climax when Garbo bought an apartment in the same building where the Schlees lived on East Fifty-second Street in New York.

Friends of Garbo's quickly noticed Schlee's influence on her. Her manner became more social, and she was taking a greater interest in life. "She responded to his forceful personality and accepted directions without questions. He also advised her on her financial affairs," one friend said. Another, commenting on Garbo's relationship to Schlee in later years, said that she looked on Schlee as "her great protector." This friend said, "He was older and wiser than most others she had known — a father-figure who looked after her, and not a lover as many believed. At times he treated her like a child. He dominated her completely and she allowed herself to be dominated by him because alone she felt always insecure. George knew her better than any other man." Perhaps Schlee's Russian background, his heavy features, and his authoritative manner carried memories of Mauritz Stiller.

Early in his friendship with Garbo, according to friends, Schlee had said to his wife, "I love her, but I'm quite sure she won't want to get married. And you and I have so much in common."

Making no attempt to conceal their unconventional relationship, Garbo and Schlee spent the summers together at Schlee's villa, Le Roc, at Cap d'Ail on the French Riviera. Outwardly gloomy, the property suited Garbo ideally; it was splendidly isolated, perched high upon jagged rocks, far from prying eyes. She went for early morning swims and sunbathed, usually topless, in a concealed part of the grounds.

When not sequestered at Le Roc, Garbo and Schlee occasionally went for short cruises on friends' yachts, including those of Aristotle Onassis and Sam Spiegel. But such excursions were infrequent. Friends recall that Schlee was "madly jealous" of Garbo, and carefully avoided allowing her to mix in the company of younger men.

Schlee died in October 1964 in Paris, where he and Garbo were staying at the Crillon on their way from the South of France. He had been in poor health for some time, and both were tired after the journey. After they checked into adjoining suites, they had an early dinner before retiring to their rooms. It was the last time Garbo saw Schlee alive. He had a heart attack in the night and died in his sleep.

On discovering his death, Garbo panicked. She packed hurriedly and fled the hotel.

For Valentina it was the end of what was left of her friendship with Garbo, and her chance for retaliation for the injuries she suffered in silence for almost twenty years. When she flew back to New York with the body of her husband, she made it clear to Garbo that she would resent her company on his last journey.

Garbo wept.

Cecil Beaton not only had a turbulent romance with Garbo, he kept a meticulous diary of the two years it lasted, portions of which appear in his autobiographical volumes.

They first met in the mid-thirties at a Hollywood party. The acquaintance was short-lived, but according to Beaton, their affair began that night.

Ten years later Beaton met Garbo again, now retired from the screen and living in New York. Neither had forgotten their first encounter. "We carried on spontaneously from where we left off — only this time for longer," Beaton wrote later. Garbo was forty-one, he forty-two, and both unmarried.

In the spring of 1946, Beaton noted: "She had never given a thought to marriage with anyone in particular. But with advancing age, she said, we become lonelier and perhaps she had made a mistake. She thought it was time to consider a lasting relationship."

I asked, "Why don't you marry me?" Garbo looked at me in astonishment and said, "You should not speak about marriage lightly." I assured her that I meant it seriously. Then she said, "You hardly know me. You would worry and not understand why I am melancholic and sad."

I asked her outright, "Do you love me?" To my surprise she said: "Yes."

After that they became inseparable, going for daily walks in Central Park, shopping, and out on the town at night.

They quarreled only when Garbo felt Beaton was asking too many questions. She resented anything that hinted at an intrusion of her privacy, even from her lover.

It was several months, said Beaton, before Garbo allowed him to visit her apartment at the Ritz Tower. "She lived like a monk with little excpet a toothbrush, a piece of soap, and a jar of face cream," he wrote.

"I usually accompanied her back to her hotel at three o'clock in the morning. Once she said, 'I wish the hours were twice as long, specially at night.' We kissed for the thousandth time — as if it were the first time."

The Christmas holidays of 1947 saw the full tide of their affair. On Christmas Day they went to a party at the home of Erich Maria Remarque. On the walk back to Garbo's hotel in the early hours of the morning, arm-in-arm along the empty street, they spoke of nothing but marriage. Beaton remembers, "I said, 'I know you don't like your first name. How would you like me to call you?' Spontaneously she answered, 'Just call me wife.' "

On New Year's Eve Garbo did a striptease for him at her hotel: "She changed into an athlete outfit, putting on tights, white socks, and red slippers. Then she took my hat and paraded around the room like a clown at a circus."

Soon afterward Beaton accompanied Garbo on a trip to Hollywood, where she told him, "This is where I have wasted the best years of my life."

When Beaton had to return to his work in England, he wanted Garbo to come with him. She refused. Describing their parting, he wrote: "I felt as if I was about to have an amputation. It was the end of a great love affair for both of us. Garbo's last words to me were, 'You see how difficult and neurotic I am. I am impossible to get on with.' I saw before me a child, its face filled with grief and sorrow."

In later years Beaton wrote about Garbo in harsh terms: "She is not interested in anything or anybody in particular. And she has become as difficult as an invalid and as selfish, quite unprepared to put herself out for anyone. She would be a trying companion, continuously sighing and full of tragic regrets. She is superstitious, suspicious, and does not know the meaning of friendship. She is incapable of love."

But her beauty was never in doubt. "Of all the women I have ever seen," he noted, "Miss Garbo is by far the most beautiful. After our first meeting in Hollywood many years passed before I met her again, but time had only improved her lunar beauty, giving her features a more chiseled sensitivity."

Eventually the two agreed to settle for friendship, and Garbo made prolonged visits to Beaton's secluded country house in the Wiltshire hills. "However, the question of our marriage did not seem to become any more positive than before," Beaton wrote. "Whenever I brought up the subject she would cast it aside or make a joke of it."

At the end of one such visit that lasted three months, the two went to Paris when Garbo wanted to do some shopping. Once there she suddenly decided that she wanted to fly back to New York. "When I joined her in New York a few weeks later," wrote Beaton, "she wouldn't answer the telephone. I could hardly believe it possible . . . after the intimacy of our times together."

Beaton published his diaries in 1973. Garbo was crushed by the act; Deborah Kerr, Salka Viertel's daughter-in-law, told me she was "deeply wounded." Commenting on Beaton's work later, a book critic for the London *Sunday Times* pointed out, "He is more of an artist than a gentleman."

Max Gumpel's daughter Laila once visited Garbo and received this advice: "Laila, promise me that you will never let money or glory rule your life. Get married and have a home and family — or you will be unhappy as I am."

But in the half century since Garbo wrote to Saxon, "I cannot see myself as a wife — ugly word," she has not changed her mind. She told me, "Not getting married was probably a mistake, but I always got scared at the last moment and ran off. At the back of my mind something always told me I would not make a good wife."

Chapter 7
MONEY

The Divine
GARBO

Chapter 7
MONEY

"No matter how much I deposit," Garbo said to a friend, "my bank balance never changes." The friend said there must be some reason for it, but Garbo couldn't figure it out.

Garbo's original contract with M-G-M was for $350 a week. At the peak of her career she received $250,000, then $270,000, then $300,000 a picture — more if shooting exceeded the schedule. For *Conquest* she received $350,000. She was a millionaire at twenty-six. Throughout her career and her retirement, she has always had the benefit of excellent advice on how to invest her earnings, and her fortune continued to grow long after she stopped working. She is today a very rich woman — one who over the years has made others rich. Her commercial value was recognized early. In 1928, on her first visit to Sweden after three years in America, she was offered 10,000 kronor for her own story. She refused. The publisher, undeterred, pursued the project and found a writer, Åke Sundborg, a Stockholm publicity man. *Greta Garbos Saga — The Story of Greta Garbo* — published in 1929 was the first book about her. A huge success, it was translated into eight languages. (Incidentally, although the twenty-three-year-old Garbo declined the role of author, she was not uncooperative. She was delighted by the cover drawing and asked to meet the artist, Einar Nerman; they have remained friends to this day.) The revivals of her movies in theaters and on television, in the United States and in Europe, have generated immense revenue; of these film festivals Garbo has claimed, "I don't get a penny out of them." The Garbo industry has now and then taken an exotic turn: mass-produced "sculptures" of her head sold well in Germany in 1933.

Garbo's first financial adviser was Mauritz Stiller, whose simple counsel had long-reaching effects. He advised Garbo from the beginning to send her savings to Sweden, where the real estate market was booming in the twenties. Garbo followed this course, and she was never to regret it. Her investments steadily grew, and by keeping only money for current expenses in her California bank, she escaped financial ruin in the crash of 1929 and the ensuing Depression.

Stiller left Hollywood in June 1927, the same month Harry Edington brilliantly negotiated Garbo's first five-year contract with M-G-M. Thanks to Stiller's advice and Edington's management, by the time it expired in 1932, Garbo had amassed a considerable — and intact — fortune.

She was reluctant to sign another contract. Her recurrent desire to leave Hollywood was strong, she had enough money, she wanted to return to Sweden, she wanted to be free. She spoke of building a house of her own on one of the tiny wooded islands off the mainland and living privately, seeing only the people she wanted to see. But the collapse of the Beverly Hills bank at just the time her contract was up for renewal was perhaps an omen. After a long holiday in Sweden, she returned to work under a new contract, lured by the financial arrangements Edington had obtained — $300,000 a picture — and the prospect of *Queen Christina*.

Harry Edington handled Garbo's financial affairs during her Hollywood years, but Garbo always heeded Stiller's early advice. She insisted on half her earnings being invested in Sweden. After paying her relatively modest living expenses, which were administered by Edington's wife, Barbara Kent, who kept track of Garbo's personal and household finances for her, Edington placed the rest in real estate in the United States. When she left Hollywood she was a millionaire several times over.

In the early forties, after leaving Hollywood and moving to New York, George Schlee took Edington's place as her financial adviser until his death in 1964. Through Schlee Garbo met Eustace Seligman, a wealthy and distinguished New York lawyer. She turned to him for counsel. She became close friends with Seligman and his wife, and the three often went out to dinner and the theatre. She also spent long weekends at the Seligmans' sprawling country estate in Greenwich, Connecticut, where she enjoyed their twenty-meter swimming pool, shut off from public view by towering trees and high hedges.

Legacies, as well as income and investments, have increased Garbo's wealth. In 1928, at Mauritz Stiller's death, she inherited half his fortune: 240,000 kronor, or $47,000 in the currency of the time.

Her largest inheritance may have come in the mid-sixties when George Schlee died. Friends of the couple say the millionaire businessman left her a large part of his estate in stocks and valuable property in Italy and the south of France. It is problematical whether he turned over to her Le Roc, the villa they had shared. Documents proving Garbo's ownership could not be produced, and Schlee's wife, Valentina, lost no time in selling the house.

The smallest such addition to her estate came when a distant relative, Carl-Gustaf Axelsson, died in 1975. Axelsson had been married to one of Garbo's aunts, and when he died at eighty-three in a village near Stockholm he left a modest estate to be divided among fourteen of his family: Garbo's share was

$750. When the administrators of the estate sought to contact the beneficiaries, no one knew Garbo's address. The case was finally referred to the Justice Department in Stockholm, leading to publication of an announcement in the form of an "open letter" to Garbo in the official journal of the Swedish Academy. This was spotted by the Swedish consulate in New York and forwarded to the actress. A lawyer, Per Danielsson, was instructed to write to Garbo, giving her further details. Shortly afterward Danielsson received a letter from Garbo stating her willingness to accept her share.

Garbo's worth is estimated conservatively by film industry experts at between $10 to $12 million; it could be much more because of constant increases in property values. According to a 1978 article in *Time*, Garbo is among those owning property on Rodeo Drive in Beverly Hills, one of the world's premier shopping avenues. Internationally famous stores vie for space, offering up to $300,000 to buy out a lease. Since 1973 rents there have tripled as oil-rich Saudis and Iranians have moved in with their petro-millions.

The question that has aroused much speculation is to whom Garbo will leave her millions. She has given the matter great thought in latter years and discussed it often with Eustace Seligman.

She has never donated to charity. Her only living family are her brother's illegitimate son, Sven Gustafsson, today a fifty-nine-year-old Swedish civil servant, and his half-sister Gray, forty-six, born of Garbo's brother's marriage to an American. Some say that Garbo's long preoccupation with health may be influential. Well-informed sources have commented on an interest in mental health and retarded children, and suggest that she will leave the bulk of her fortune to these causes. Only one thing is clear: "She has turned down vehemently a proposal for the creation of a 'Greta Garbo Foundation,' " a friend said. "She wants her name to become extinct with her death."

CLOSE-UP

The Divine GARBO

Chapter 8
CLOSE-UP

"I am forever running away from something or somebody," Garbo told me in the summer of 1977. "Subconsciously I have always known that I was not destined for real and lasting happiness."

From her recurring remarks in our time together, the pattern of Garbo's concept of a "happy life" emerged: a little house somewhere in the country with a fireplace "for sitting around and dreaming," simple food, and a good friend by her side who wouldn't talk too much or question her thoughts. She longs to be understood without words and free to do as she pleases without the need for excuses or explanations.

But Garbo herself has put up insurmountable barriers between herself and this "happy life." Her self-imposed isolation, her constant quest for privacy, her distrust of people, made her few friends. And for some of those friends she did make, her expectations were too high to be fulfilled.

The Garbo I met still recoils at the sight of strangers, and by her own admission the world's most famous living legend is leading a lonely and unhappy life. When I asked her if she was happy to be back in Europe, she said, "Happiness, what is that? I have never known it." She arouses pity and sympathy easily and reveals a distinct craving for affection.

Her childhood was clouded by poverty; as an adult she knew neither home nor family life. Disliking domesticity in any shape or form, she never wanted a permanent home of her own, preferring to live in rented houses or hotels. During her sixteen years in Hollywood she moved eleven times; she looks upon possessions, from cigarette lighters to houses, as "millstones around one's neck."

Today, she genuinely prefers her seclusion, which was, after all, not forced on her but created by her own will. Her shyness is not feigned, and she truly wants to be alone in a dream world of her own choice. It is her escape from the realities of a life in which she has found little joy. But even her closest friends are in doubt as to what she has gained by it. They question whether hers is a rich dream life, a brooding over the past, or sheer boredom.

Of Klosters in Switzerland, Garbo told me, "Fate has chained me here," referring to her yearly visits to her old friend Salka Viertel, then an invalid. Not that Garbo enjoys living in New York any better: "Sure, there is good theatre and opera, but as I don't go out in the evenings, what good is it to me? I might as well be living on a desert island. The climate is awful here, but so it is in New York. Where is it good, can you tell me? I am restless everywhere, and always have been. So that won't change wherever I might go." Resignedly she added, "So what's the good of caring?" Now that Salka Viertel is dead, will Garbo keep coming to Klosters? She has met people here with whom she is comfortable, and the quiet days here are not unlike the "happy life" she has described. As for Sweden, she told me, "I love my country and would dearly like to go back one day, but the mob scenes on my last visit still scare me when I think of it."

She takes a jaundiced view of life, characterized by her recurrent use in conversation of the German word *verwahrlost*, meaning neglected, unkempt, depraved. "*Alles ist verwahr-lost,*" Garbo will say several times a day, referring to anything from the weather to international affairs. "The whole world is *verwahrlost,*" she said to me. "Why can't the cleverest men of all countries get together and use their brains to make it a peaceful world? Why must there always be troubles and tensions somewhere? *Ach, alles ist verwahrlost.*" Although Garbo complained to me often of loneliness and boredom and spoke of her "wasted life," she has steadfastly resisted throughout her long retirement engaging in any kind of welfare or charitable activity. Her profession was actress, not social worker.

Garbo's small, nondescript apartment in Klosters is near the center of town. She spends her days mostly walking, reading, waiting — "I don't really know for what." The apartment has a twenty-eight-foot terrace on which she does a daily forty-five minutes of exercises and jogging before breakfast, and she generally takes long walks twice a day.

Although her back bothers her occasionally, her health is excellent; but it is never far from her thoughts, and she takes good care of herself. Still, she is a smoker, often lighting four or five of her black cigarettes in a row. She made an unsuccessful effort some ten years ago to break the habit and consulted a specialist in Zurich who claimed he could cure anyone of smoking by hypnosis. "I went to him full of good intentions of giving it up," she told me, "but he imposed one condition. I was not to have a cigarette for four days after treatment. He even made me a bet that if I held out those four days, I would lose all desire to smoke. I really believed him and followed his instructions. On the fifth day I lit up again, unable to restrain myself any longer. Since then I have never been able to stop. Now I can't even be bothered to try." She is more disciplined about alcohol. She told me, "I love a drink myself. But unfortunately I have to restrict myself to one whiskey a day." Her body is strong and is in good shape, but through the years she has suffered from insomnia and exhaustion, complaints which sometimes have a nervous origin. Her concern with health — or illness — may not be unrelated to her early experiences of the sickness and death of those close to her: her father died after a long illness when she was fourteen; her sister died at twenty-two, when Garbo was twenty; Mauritz Stiller died three years later.

Despite Garbo's preoccupation with her health, however, she no longer is particularly concerned about "health foods." Each day in Klosters, shortly before the shops close at noon and thus can be relied on to be empty, she slips into the grocer's opposite her apartment house and buys her simple, not to say meager, ration of food for the day: fruit, salad, occasionally pasta. "You should see how I eat and what I eat," she told me. "I have no idea of cooking and am much too lazy to look at a cookbook."

She is a simple person by nature, and in a casual meeting does not attempt to impress a new acquaintance. But then, she does not need to: no one can approach Garbo without awe, and surely she knows that. She exaggerates her simplicity of dress and manner. She knows she can look more luminous in a sack than most women bedecked in sables, and she prefers to wear slacks and sweaters rather than the smart clothes designed for her by New York's top couturiers. Her constant attempts in public situations to avoid drawing attention to herself have on more than one occasion produced the opposite effect.

Garbo herself distrusts the evocative quality of her own beauty. She has always been wary of compliments, much as an heiress is suspicious of suitors. Her wariness had two results, neither of them happy: her relationships with other people were burdened by distrust, and her public image as a "woman of mystery" — who is then of course an object of curiosity — was strengthened. Nor did the adoration she inspired ever sit comfortably or gracefully on her shoulders, like the honor earned that it was. She was regarded as a goddess by her public and as a property by M-G-M, and she sought to avoid both roles by secrecy, withdrawal, and wide-brimmed hats.

"If you are Garbo's friend and would remain so, you've got to take the oath of silence." This contemporary observation of Garbo in her Hollywood days has remained true all her life, and breaking the oath is never forgiven. Cecil Beaton was the most notable of the offenders, but there have been others who destroyed their relationship with Garbo by talking or writing about her, including Mercedes de Acosta. Garbo felt that they had exploited her friendship, and she retaliated by banishing them from her circle. Those of her friends who did discuss her with us did so only on condition that they not be quoted by name. Garbo claims that everything written about her is wrong or fabrication, that nobody knows her and therefore all is conjecture. "I never talk to the press, so how should they know?" she reasonably pointed out. She professes never to read anything about herself.

Only Garbo's nephew, Sven Gustafsson, broke his silence to talk at length about his family in an interview with Sven Broman. Mr. Gustafsson is the illegitimate son of Garbo's brother Sven; he was born when Garbo was fourteen. He was brought up in the Gustafsson family's small apartment at Blekingegatan 32. Today a civil servant, Mr. Gustafsson lives comfortably in a residential suburb of Stockholm, surrounded by souvenirs and photos of Garbo that were left to him by his father. He told Broman:

My parents were never married. They separated when I was nine. Later my father married an American girl, Marguerite Balzer, known as "Peggy." They had a daughter, Gray, born in 1932, who is married to an American gynecologist and lives in New Jersey. Today she and I are Garbo's nearest living relatives.

Greta made my father promise never to talk about our family and especially not about her. For many years I also respected her wish, but I feel no longer bound by it. Not only are my father and mother

148

now dead a long time, but Greta has never answered any of my letters.

I have never asked her for anything. It may be that she feared I would take after my father, who failed in everything he ever did and relied heavily on his rich sister's support.

More than anything Greta was always afraid that anyone would talk about her origins and the true extent of her family's poverty, like the seven of us living in one room.

I remember my father telling me that when Greta's sister, Alva, was asked out to dinner one evening, her mother told her, "Be sure to eat everything you can, because there will be very little to eat tomorrow." My father told many stories about Greta in her youth when she was a shop assistant at PUB and had a boyfriend, Max Gumpel, who was a good deal older than she.

Once he sent her a beautiful blouse and telephoned shortly afterward to invite her out. The way father told it, she thanked him for the blouse but said she couldn't go out because she had no skirt to wear with it. Then Gumpel appeared at the doorstep, carrying a matching skirt. He waited outside while she changed. But Greta was furious that he had come to her home and seen how she lived.

My parents separated in the late twenties and I stayed with my father in a small but artistically decorated apartment on two floors. When Greta came to Sweden on her first visit from Hollywood in 1928 she stayed with us for a few days.

She was very nice to me and gave me a big Meccano construction set for Christmas. I was only nine at the time, but I remember how indescribably beautiful she was. One day she took me to the railway station when I went to visit my grandmother, and I was very proud to be seen with her.

In 1939, shortly before the outbreak of World War II, Garbo brought her mother to America. Afraid of being cut off from his sister by the war, Sven followed with his wife and seven-year-old daughter. But after six months in California Sven moved with his mother and his family to Santa Fe, New Mexico, where the climate would be better for his mother, who suffered from rheumatism. She died in Santa Fe in 1944, and Sven arranged for her burial in Sweden. On behalf of his sister Greta, Sven had purchased a family plot in Södra Skogskyrkogården (South Forest Churchyard) in Stockholm. A granite gravestone bears the simple inscription "Gustafsons Familjegrav," marking the graves of Garbo's father, mother, and sister; a place remains for Greta. Yellow violets, sent from New York, decorate the grave every Mother's Day — in Sweden the last Sunday in May — as part of Garbo's standing orders for its care and maintenance. The spelling of Gustafson on the stone reflects her brother's Americanization; he changed it from the more "foreign" Gustafsson when he came to the United States. Sven is buried in Santa Fe, where he died in 1967.

I saw Garbo just before her seventy-second birthday, and it was apparent that she still keeps her inner life as secret as she did fifty years ago. It is unlikely that anyone has ever truly understood the workings of her mind. She is no intellectual and has always felt uneasy about her lack of formal academic education, but she possesses a sound natural intelligence. One friend said, "Greta would have made a very good psychotherapist. She has her own kind of special magic therapy. One is forever conscious of it in her company." I experienced that "magic" even in telephone conversations with Garbo, occasions when she is at her most maddeningly mysterious.

Garbo never answers the telephone at all unless she expects someone she wishes to talk to to call her at a prearranged hour. Even then, she cannot be said to "answer" the telephone: she simply picks up the receiver and waits for the caller to speak first. It is an awesome experience for the uninitiated, but her friends know her habit and accept it. Once in conversation, Garbo will talk as long — or as briefly — as it suits her, which can be thirty seconds or half an hour, depending on her mood. Once I bade her good night at the end of an evening telephone conversation, innocently adding, "Sleep well."

Garbo immediately reproached me. "Don't say that," she said. " 'Good night' is enough. I'm full of taboos. Now I'll lie awake all night and think about having to 'sleep well.' "

Garbo is a better listener than she is a talker; when she talks her conversation is mostly about herself, but, one quickly realizes, without telling you very much. She can laugh heartily, and is apparently sincere in what she says. She takes an intense interest in the lives of others, particularly people she knows, and she enjoys hearing the latest gossip. She has a pixie sense of humor and an appreciation of the ridiculous. She can display a charming childlike delight when she is amused or pleased; at such times she sits with her hands clasped together between her knees. On the other hand, there is little humor in her melancholic moods, when she will tell you that her life is over, that all she did was "make a mess of it from start to finish."

Garbo is a woman whose company one enjoys when the time and place are right and she is in the right mood. She can also be willful and difficult. She avoids making decisions, even the most trivial, such as in which direction to go for a walk with a companion. Although most of the time she doesn't know what to do from one hour to the next, she won't commit herself to a plan or invitation. She will speculate about what she will do tomorrow, only to change her mind when tomorrow comes. Friends complain that she will never make an appointment more than an hour beforehand; if she accepts an invitation she is unpredictable about how long she will stay. "You ask her for dinner and she may leave suddenly after a couple of drinks, or not arrive until dinner is over," one exasperated New York hostess said.

When I was in Klosters, Garbo asked me to take her on a shopping trip to St. Moritz, a three-hour drive. She spoke about the trip at length: she knew which shops she wanted to go to, where to have lunch. The conversation moved on to travel in general, and I told her about a spot by the sea near

Athens where I had recently spent a vacation. She liked the sound of it and said, "In that case, Sandy, let's go there instead of St. Moritz." By morning she had changed her mind about both destinations: "There may be too many people," she said.

So we shopped at Davos, where Garbo looked at slacks, sweaters, and scarves in a dozen or so shops. Garbo often window-shops, and she had seen all the displays before, but had been too shy to go inside the stores. This time not being alone gave her confidence. In some of the stores she was recognized, not in others. After much deliberation Garbo decided to buy a navy blue blouse and a pair of long woolen stockings. She made her purchases at the shop where she was fussed over the most. When at last we went for coffee, she said, "I don't usually buy anything that quickly. I hope I did the right thing."

Although Garbo enjoys travel and of course is now free to go wherever and whenever her fancy takes her, she is a prisoner of her own fears. The train trip from Klosters to Davos takes twenty-five minutes; it was two years before Garbo could manage to do it. As we drove past the railway station at Davos she told me how she had often wanted to make the trip but had lacked the courage. "Many times I went to the station and turned back at the last moment," she said. "Heaven knows how many tickets I bought, but each time the train pulled into the station I was frightened and walked away. It took me two years before I finally ventured on it the first time."

She fears crowds, and she fears recognition. Therefore whenever she plans a trip she is faced with a difficult decision. She knows that if she travels as herself she will be given VIP treatment and unwanted attentions, but she will have nothing to do but sit back and relax. If she travels under a false name she will be exposed to crowds, confusion, and the usual discomforts and inconveniences encountered by the ordinary traveler. Her back prevents her from picking anything up, and because she might not find a porter she never travels by train when she has luggage.

Garbo enjoys traveling by car, but this too presents problems. She told me, "I wish I could drive, then I could travel more. As it is I have to depend on friends to take me out every now and then." The situation is not made easier by her unwillingness to make plans ahead.

On the last full day of my visit I saw again Garbo's difficulty in coping with ordinary life. That morning we had driven from Klosters and walked around Lake Davos; now we were stopping for lunch in the town. She sincerely wanted to be unnoticed and unrecognized, yet because she couldn't decide which table she preferred, she stood endlessly in the middle of the crowded restaurant while she tried to make up her mind. Needless to say, by the time she made her choice everyone in the place had noticed and recognized her.

Once settled, she studied the menu in thoughtful silence. After what seemed an interminable time she announced that she wanted neither meat nor fish. I suggested a spaghetti dish, but Garbo shook her head. "No spaghetti for me," she said. "I have it at home all the time. It's one of the few things I know how to do myself." Finally she decided on a salad and ham and eggs. I did not ask if she could not do that at home.

When the check arrived, Garbo wanted to pay her share. "Why should men always pay for women?" she asked.

"Do you believe in women's lib?" I teased.

"Not really," she said. "Not when I see what most of them look like."

Despite the cold weather and intermittent cloudbursts, Garbo suggested we drive back to the lake and walk off our meal. With a smile she joked, "I won't walk you around for a second time. Halfway will do."

A men's choir was lined up outside the restaurant, singing lustily. On other occasions Garbo would have fled back inside to hide, but this time she stood quite near them, listening until the end, when she clapped with delight.

Back in the car, though, she seemed to grow sad, and I asked if anything was wrong.

"I've messed up my life," she said, "and it's too late to change that. You see, these walks are only an escape. When I walk alone I think about my life and the past. There is a lot to think back on. I am not satisfied with the way I made my life."

But she did not dwell on this theme; instead, as we began to walk, she asked me questions about myself and about the celebrities I had encountered in my work. Of all those we talked about she was particularly interested to hear about C. G. Jung, the Aga Khan, and Charlie and Oona Chaplin. She asked me many questions about the Chaplins, mostly about Oona. "What kind of a life has she had since she married a man so much older than herself?" she wanted to know. "Does she really like children so much as to have had so many?" It soon became apparent, however, that these questions about Oona were not the central ones. Earlier I had asked Garbo if she had ever thought about writing her life story, and she had said she wouldn't know how; I had told her Oona Chaplin was working on hers. Now she wanted me to tell her what Oona is really like, and finally she asked if I believed she had the capability of writing a book. I assured her I did; and I could see this gave Garbo food for thought.

Garbo is a revolutionary in many ways. She swims against the tide, she is a nonconformist (or rather she does not conform to the ideas others have of her and of what she "should" do). She has always resented the cheap sentiment of most of her roles on the screen, and she dislikes sentimentality in any form; yet she is capable of moaning "*Alles ist verwahrlost*" at the least provocation.

Garbo's physical mystery — and mastery — still apparent today, was not the creation of the wizards of Hollywood. Although they cast her in stereotyped roles, they could not diminish her ability to entrance both men and women. Garbo's inescapable magnetism could not be defined, but it could be exploited. And whatever private grief it may have cost her when she built her wall around herself and let the world regard her as an enigma if not an outright curiosity, she has never let herself be exploited again.

Garbo's relationship with her audiences has always been immediate and direct. Some actresses have used a strong single attribute to make themselves memorable: a dramatic vocal instrument, a sensitive interpretive ability, a beguiling presence. Garbo in fact had these; but her great achievement was to know, whether instinctively or through training, to act not with but through her remarkable face. Her beauty was innate and alive, so that even in complete repose she conveyed an immense sweep of suggestion. She never had to cheat in her physical relationship with an audience. And, consciously or not, her audiences knew this, and responded to her as to no other actress. Perhaps the adoration that such honesty provoked made relationships in her personal life more difficult to achieve, or depend on.

Garbo's was a face that seemed to have its own life, a life that no make-up man could — or should ever have wanted to — alter. Her mysterious alchemy required no artifice, and she could evoke profound reactions even through the barriers of second-rate scripts. She knew she had something, although no one could say exactly what it was. Sometimes it frightened her, because she had not created it, it was not in her control, and she knew that she was not the marble goddess to whom she was so often compared. But that of course was the wonderful secret: that no matter how perfect her face, it was *not* marble, but human and alive — and so it held the promise of telling us, at any moment, all we could ever want to know about Anna Christie or Ninotchka or Camille. That face — so beautiful — was open to us, and we could read in it all our dreams. Her wisest directors knew this, and knew, as did Garbo herself, that her greatest strength lay in the close-up.

But even Garbo's unequivocal beauty is not without paradox. Once her adolescent plumpness had gone, never to return, her body was strong and attractive. Yet, possibly because of the unearthly radiance of her face and what it could convey, her body by contrast has been described, from her childhood into her lean and graceful seventies, as ungainly, gangling, flat-footed, rawboned, dowdy. On screen she did not move like a goddess, or even like an actress; she moved like herself, or, more to the point, like Mata Hari or Susan Lenox. Her movements are often brisk, giving the impression of wanting to get things done, revealing an amalgam of impetuous child and self-assured woman. Even those who have known her have fallen into the trap of describing her as "athletic" or "statuesque," perhaps in an attempt to come up with images that fit one's notion of a Norse goddess. But she is not particularly tall, and her feet are size six. The myth of Garbo's big feet can be credited to gossip columnists caught between a subject who would not chat with them and a public always demanding to know more about the "Swedish sphinx." True, before a scene was shot Garbo always asked her cameraman, "Is the feets in?" But her concern was not to conceal her feet if the answer was yes, but simply to change out of the bedroom slippers she wore for comfort under even the most ornate costume.

That face. One keeps coming back to that face. To see Garbo's face in a film made when she was thirty is to understand that she could never age as the rest of us do. The radiance from her beacon eyes at once told all, promised everything; they were trusting like a child's, knowing like a woman's, forgiving like a mother's. The incredibly long lashes that innocently but inescapably hint at seduction. The mouth, flexible, full, sculptured, the upper lip flashing private messages of decisiveness and strength, the lower lip echoing lurking sensuality. The heavy eyelids, the translucent skin over wide cheekbones that gave Garbo the uncanny ability to create mood and tension with the slightest flicker. Garbo and her best directors knew that in close-ups she did not have to move her head to achieve a desired reaction — remember the close-up at the end of *Queen Christina*. No, they knew better than that. They knew that it is not even a question of "achieving," but of revealing, and so they knew not to get in the way, by any superfluous movement or false emotion, of the truth the audience would see when they looked at her face. That was her impact and her gift — to bring others to the point of true identification with the woman they saw on the screen, as their unconscious responded to, resonated with hers. How that happens, of course, is the true mystery of Garbo, and of art.

Index

A HORRID FACTBOOK

HORRID HENRY'S BODIES

Francesca Simon
Illustrated by Tony Ross

Orion
Children's Books

First published in Great Britain in 2011
by Orion Children's Books
a division of the Orion Publishing Group Ltd
Orion House
5 Upper Saint Martin's Lane
London WC2H 9EA
An Hachette UK Company

1 3 5 7 9 10 8 6 4 2

Text © Francesca Simon 2011
Illustrations © Tony Ross 2011

ISBN 978 1 4440 0162 4

A catalogue record for this book is available from the British Library.

Printed in Great Britain by
Clays Ltd, St Ives plc

www.orionbooks.co.uk

www.horridhenry.co.uk

CONTENTS

Hello from Henry

Hold on tight, everyone, you are about to open the grisliest, grossest, most disgusting book ever! And it's all true, so your mean, horrible parents can't complain when you tell them all about bogies, earwax, mucus, wee or head lice. You name it, you'll find all the facts you need to know to gross out your teachers and revolt your friends. Yippee!

Henry

BLECCCH!
FOUL FACTS

The **loudest burp** recorded (so far) was 107.1 decibels – that's louder than the sound of a drill breaking up concrete!

When you sneeze, the air coming out of your nose and mouth travels at 100 miles per hour – even faster than cars on a motorway.

Did you know that you produce more than a litre of saliva every day?

Your nose also makes about a litre of **slimy glop** each day – called mucus. And most of it, you swallow. Eeew!

On a normal day, you produce about half a litre of sweat. But if it's hot and you do lots of exercise, you could produce up to seven litres. That's three and a half big bottles of fizzywizz!

The sweatiest part of your body isn't your armpits or your feet – it's the palms of your hands.

What's in a **bogey**? Dried mucus mixed with dust and dirt – with a few bugs to add extra flavour!

Can you believe it? You'll spend three years of your life on the toilet.

You produce about 45,000 litres of urine in a lifetime – enough to fill 450 baths.

Romans used to brush their teeth with urine. **Bleccccch!**

Ever tried beetroot? If you eat too much of it, your wee will turn pink!

When an astronaut spacewalks on the moon, he wears something called a Maximum Absorption Garment. Sounds grand but it's really a **man-sized nappy**.

Long ago in the Fourteenth Century, it wasn't cool to wash, so people sprayed on lots of perfume to cover their **stinky smell** instead.

When you die, your skin shrinks and this makes your nails and hair look as though they're still growing. **Scary!**

Ancient Egyptians used to cut open a dead body, remove the insides and place them in a jar next to the coffin. Then they made a mummy by bandaging the body up in strips of linen.

Whenever you talk or chew, little clumps of **earwax** fall out of your ears. Luckily, they are too small to see.

INSIDE
INFO

If you could touch your brain, it would feel like **jelly**.

Just because your brain is small, doesn't mean you're not as clever as someone with a big brain.

Did you know that nearly two-thirds of your body is made up of water?

In your lifetime, your heart will beat about **2,500 million times** – and never take a rest.

Try clenching your fist — it's about the same size of your heart. As you get older and your fist grows bigger, so does your heart.

Your liver is the **largest** and **heaviest** organ inside your body, weighing an average of 1.6 kilograms. That's the same as three bags of pasta!

If your **blood vessels** were all stretched out like a piece of string, they would circle around the Earth twice.

It takes only one minute for a drop of blood to travel all around your body.

If you were ill in the Middle Ages, the doctor might have put **leeches** on your body to suck some of the blood out for you.

I wonder why they didn't try nits...

Our bodies are always 37°C – it doesn't matter if the weather's hot or cold. But cold-blooded animals like lizards have to warm themselves up in the sun.

Your smallest muscle is called the **stapedius** – it's in your ear and it helps to protect you from loud noises.

And your biggest muscle is in your
bottom and is called the **gluteus maximus**.

There are more than **60 muscles** in your
face – that's why you can make lots of
funny expressions.

You use about **40 muscles to frown**, but only about 20 to smile. Being moody like Margaret must be very tiring!

Did you know you use 90 muscles in your leg every time you take a step?

Do you ever get **butterflies** in your tummy? If you're frightened or worried, the muscles in your tummy suddenly shorten and you get this funny fluttering feeling.

Ever put a shell to your ear and heard the sound of the sea? What you're really hearing are **sound waves** bouncing between the shell, your ear lobes, the inside of your ear and your eardrum.

If you took out your intestines and uncoiled them, they'd be about **four times** as tall as you.

Did you know that your stomach is full of strong acid that turns your food into liquid?

Just think how much is sloshing around in Greedy Graham's guts.

You breathe in and out about 15 times every minute – that's about 20,000 times a day. **Phew!**

BRILLIANT
BONES

There are **206 bones** in an adult human skeleton.

As a newborn baby you have even more bones (up to 270) but many of them fuse together as you get older.

If you didn't have a skeleton, your body would collapse into a **shapeless lump**.

Did you know that your longest bone is in your thigh and is called the femur? It's roughly a quarter of your total height.

Can you bend any of your joints so far the wrong way that they look broken? If you can then you're **double-jointed**.

Your **smallest bone** is in your ear. It's called the stirrup bone and it's smaller than a grain of rice.

Measure your height in the morning and then again in the evening – you'll find you're smaller in the evening. This is the effect of **gravity** on your spine. Don't worry, during the night you'll go back to your full height again.

We all have 12 pairs of ribs, but about one person in five hundred has an extra one – lucky them!

Have you found your **funny bone**? It isn't really a bone – it's a nerve on your elbow. If you've ever banged it by mistake, you'll find that it isn't really funny either – it hurts!

In 3000 BC, doctors performed brain surgery on their patients by drilling a hole in their skulls – just to see what happened!

I wonder what you'd see if you drilled a hole in Margaret's skull...

SKIN,
SCALES AND
SCABS

Your skin is your heaviest and largest organ.
An adult's skin weighs about four kilograms –
the same weight as two big bottles of fizzywizz.

If a grown-up took off his skin and ironed
it flat, it would be about the **size of a
single bed**.

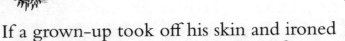

Your thinnest skin – 0.5mm – is on your
eyelids.

Your thickest skin – 5mm thick and more – is
on the soles of your feet.

Your skin might look and feel smooth, but
really it's covered in lumps, bumps, ridges and
grooves where **billions of body bugs** hide.
Yeuch!

You've heard about snakes shedding their scaly skins – well, you do too! Every minute, about **50,000** tiny flakes of skin fall off your body.

Every month your body makes a new skin, and during your lifetime you'll have about 1,000 new skins.

If your dead skin cells didn't drop off, after three years your skin would be as thick as an **elephant's**.

When you cut yourself, your blood thickens to form a scab. The scab stops germs getting into the cut while your skin heals, so don't pick at it!

If you have a cut that's producing a thick yellow pus, act fast! It means that **germs** have got in, and your cut needs cleaning.

Do you like carrots?
Be careful, if you eat
too many of them, your
skin might **turn orange**.

If you ever need stitches, the doctor might use something called cat gut. But don't worry, it isn't really cat gut – it's made from sheep or goat intestines … so that's OK then!

HORRIBLY
HAIRY
FACTS

Did you know that you're just as hairy as a gorilla? Luckily your body hair is much shorter and thinner!

Unless of course you're Bossy Bill or Stuck-Up Steve.

Have you noticed that you're hairy all over apart from a few places? Only the soles of your feet and the palms of your hands are hair-free.

About 100 hairs fall out of your head every day. But don't worry, new ones grow to replace them all the time!

Too bad that's not true for Mr Mossy. Tee hee.

Your hair and nails might look and feel very different, but they're made of the same stuff – something called **keratin**.

Hair grows faster at night and also faster in the summer – strange but true!

Ever wondered what your eyebrows are for? They help stop sweat dropping into your eyes.

Eyebrows show people how you're feeling. If you raise them you look surprised, if you lower them, you look puzzled, and if you lower them right down, you look angry.

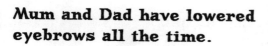

Mum and Dad have lowered eyebrows all the time.

When you're cold, you get **goose pimples** and your body hairs stand on end. This traps air and helps keep your body warm.

Your hair stands on end when you're frightened. In Prehistoric times, this **hair-raising effect** was supposed to make us look bigger to frighten our enemies.

Men have more nose hair than women ... and it grows longer and longer as they get older.

Wow! A woman in China grew her hair to 5.6 metres – the longest ever recorded. If she leaned out of a window on the second floor of a house, her hair would touch the ground.

The **longest beard** ever measured was only
a little bit shorter than the record-breaking
hair, at 5.33 metres long.

An Indian man grew the
longest ear hair ever –
18.1cm. It sprouted out of
the middle of his ears, and
hung right down to his
shoulders.

When Elizabeth I was Queen of England,
it was the fashion for ladies to pluck out
some of their hair to make their foreheads
look very high.

I bet you didn't know that whales have hair too – not very much though.

If you're fair-haired you have about **130,000 hairs** on your head – quite a lot more than your brown, black or red-haired friends.

Do you ever brush your hair? In Victorian times, you'd have been told to brush it a hundred times a day.

Boring. I'm glad I'm not a Victorian.

EYES
IN-DEPTH

Around **80**% of people have brown eyes.
The rest have blue, green, hazel or grey eyes.

Most babies are born with blue eyes, but
not many stay blue. Most of them change
to brown, hazel, grey or green.

Your pupils, the black spots in the centre
of your eyes, are really holes that let in light,
which is why they get bigger in the dark and
smaller in the bright sunshine.

If you see someone you like, your heart beats
faster and this makes your pupils get bigger too.

Cats can see better than humans in the dark because their pupils let in more light, and they also use their whiskers to find their way about.

Unless of course your cat is like Fat Fluffy, who never moves.

Owls can see well at night too because they have very big pupils.

Owls can't move their eyes like we can. They can move their whole heads almost right round instead.

Rabbits and parrots can see behind themselves without turning their heads.

Squids have the largest eyes. They are 25cm across – as large as a dinner plate.

In your lifetime, you will blink **415 million times**.

If you live to 75, you'll have cried 12 buckets worth of tears.

Lots of animals cry tears when they're in pain, but only humans cry tears when they are upset.

Even Weepy William would find it impossible to cry in space – **no gravity** means your tears won't trickle.

Gorgeous Gurinder's long eyelashes are very good at doing their job – stopping dust, dirt and insects from getting in her eyes.

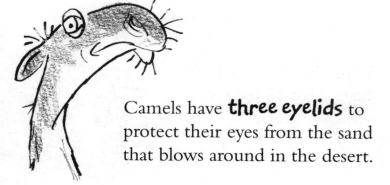

Camels have **three eyelids** to protect their eyes from the sand that blows around in the desert.

Did you know that strong sunshine can damage your eyes? You should always wear sunglasses and never look directly at the sun.

Even when a snake has its eyes closed, it can still see through its eyelids. **Sneaky!**

TERRIBLE TONGUES

The average length of a human tongue
is 10cm from the back of the throat to the
tip of the tongue.

A giraffe has such a long
tongue – 53cm – that it can
clean its own ears.

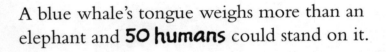

A blue whale's tongue weighs more than an
elephant and **50 humans** could stand on it.

Crocodiles can't move their tongues and they
can't chew – but they can swallow . . .

A chameleon's tongue is nearly twice the length of its body. It shoots in and out to catch insects so fast that we can't see it happen.

Snakes smell with their tongues. When they flick their tongues in and out, they are sniffing out food and danger.

A giraffe's tongue is **bluish-black** in colour – to stop it getting sunburned while the giraffe eats.

Your tongue has about 10,000 tiny taste buds, but they are so small you can't see them.

Over the years, some taste buds die and are not replaced. So kids have the best taste buds.

No wonder Mum and Dad like sprouts so much!

When you're really old, you might catch an infection called **black hairy tongue**. Your taste buds swell up and go a funny colour, and your tongue looks dark and furry.

Or you could be Margaret and have it now.

HANDY
FACTS

Your **fingerprints** are formed when you're just three months old inside your mum's tummy.

Your fingerprints are completely unique. Even identical twins have different prints.

One person in ten is left-handed, and boys are more likely to be left-handed than girls.

If you're left-handed, the nails on your left hand grow faster than the ones on your right.

And if you're right-handed, the nails on your right hand grow faster than those on your left.

Some people can write just as well with both their hands — this is called being **ambidextrous**.

Most nails grow 0.5 millimetres each week.

Some people never cut their nails – and nails have been known to grow up to 90cm long.

If you bite your nails – be warned! There are more germs under your fingernails than **under the toilet seat**.

SUPER
SENSES

We have **five senses** – touch, taste, sight, smell and hearing.

Your senses of smell and taste work together. If something smells bad, you won't like the taste of it – this stops you eating mouldy or poisonous food.

Some people have **synaesthesia**, which means their senses are mixed up. They hear colours, feel sights and smell tastes.

If you're colour-blind, you can't tell the difference between red and green.

More boys than girls are colour-blind.

Some people suffer from total colour blindness
and see everything in shades of grey – like an
old black=and-white film.

Most mammals see the world in **black**
and **white**.

Moles live underground, and they have poor
eyesight, so they use touch and smell to find
their food.

Did you know that your nose can remember
more than **10,000 different smells**?

Your sense of touch is felt by your
nerve-endings, particularly on your tongue,
lips and fingertips.

Bats use sound to see
in the dark. When
they squeak, the sound
waves hit whatever's in
front of them, and bounce
back to their ears like **an echo**.

Your taste buds recognise four basic tastes:
salty, sweet, bitter (like coffee) and sour
(like lemons).

Have you heard of **ultrasound**? Some
animals, like dogs, cats, dolphins, bats and
mice can hear ultrasound, but it's too high
for human ears.

SNOOZE
NEWS

You're probably going to spend about one-third of your life asleep.

Lazy Linda spends about two-thirds of hers asleep!

The average person falls asleep in **seven minutes**.

Getting lots of sleep helps you grow.

Your brain needs to rest too – which is why if you don't get enough sleep, you'll get **very moody**!

A newborn baby sleeps for 20 hours a day, while a ten year old sleeps for around ten hours.

Just like Lazy Linda, some animals love to sleep. Pythons sleep for 18 hours a day, tigers for 16 and cats for 12.

Fat Fluffy sleeps 24 hours a day.

Snails sometimes sleep for three years.

Every year, you have about 1,000 dreams. Most of them, you'll forget.

Cows can sleep standing up, but they can only dream lying down.

The **loudest snore** ever recorded was 93 decibels – that's louder than the sound of the traffic on the motorway!

That's almost how loud New Nick snored when I had a sleepover at his house.

The current record for going without sleep is 11 days. **Yawn!**

AMAZING ANIMALS

There are **100,000 muscles** in an elephant's trunk, while you have only 650 skeletal muscles in your whole body.

Under all their fluffy white fur, polar bears actually have black skin.

Most tigers have more than 100 stripes, and every tiger has a different pattern.

If you shaved off a tiger's stripy fur, you'd discover that it has **stripy skin** too.

Flamingos are born grey and white – it's all
the shrimp they eat that turns them pink.

A hippopotamus can open its mouth
1.2 metres wide – just about enough to
fit in a ten-year-old boy or girl.

**I wonder if I could trick Stuck-Up Steve
or Moody Margaret into going near one?**

The **most venomous** spider
in the world is the Brazilian
Wandering Spider – just
the tiniest drop of its
venom can kill a mouse.

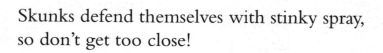

Skunks defend themselves with stinky spray,
so don't get too close!

Cobras protect themselves by shooting poison into their enemies' eyes and blinding them for a while. It's very painful too!

To scare off enemies, the horned lizard **squirts blood** from its eyelids.

That's brilliant. Wish I could.

The only bird that can **fly backwards** is the hummingbird.

Bats are the only mammals that can fly.

The largest frog is about 30cm long, and the smallest is less than 2cm.

Frogs don't drink water – they absorb it through their skin.

Shrews eat their own **body weight** in food every day.

Even Greedy Graham can't do that, though he tries . . .

An ostrich egg weighs well over a kilo – it would take 40 minutes to hard-boil it.

The Ancient Greeks used to blow up a **pig's bladder** and play football with it.

A rhinoceros's horn might look as though it's made of bone, but it's actually made out of hair.

DEEP-SEA
DATA

A blue whale's heart is the size of a small car.

If a shark is charging at you, it can't stop — it can only swerve to one side.

Sharks can't swim backwards.

The largest jellyfish ever found was 2.3 metres long — even longer than your bed.

Sharks can **smell blood** in the water up to five kilometres away.

The blue whale can make an ear-splitting 188 decibel sound. That's nearly twice as loud as a road drill and it can be heard underwater over 800 kilometres away.

When a puffer fish is scared, it swallows water or air and blows itself up into a big, spiny ball.

If a shark stops beating its tail, it will sink.

An octopus has three hearts.

If a starfish loses an arm, it can grow another one.

Emperor penguins can stay under water for an amazing **11 minutes**. The human record for staying underwater is 7.5 minutes – which is also very impressive.

Sometimes sharks go to sleep at night on the sea floor. **Aah!**

CRAZY
CREEPY-
CRAWLIES

Bedbugs hate the sunshine, so they come out and bite you at night.

Head lice love **sucking blood** from your scalp. But don't panic, they're so tiny you won't feel a thing.

Sometimes head lice are so greedy that they drink too much of your blood, their stomachs spring a leak and they die. What a shame!

Female head lice glue their eggs to
your hair using a special super-strong
glue. Even if you wash your hair or go
swimming, those eggs will stay stuck!

A broad tapeworm can grow inside your
intestine for years, reaching a length of
ten metres. **Aaagh!**

Buzzy insects like bees don't make noises
with their voices – but by moving their
wings very quickly.

A leech will gorge itself on blood
until it is **five times bigger** than when
it started.

A caterpillar has more muscles in its body than Aerobic Al (or anyone else!).

Cockroaches can flatten themselves and slide into tiny cracks in the wall.

A slug can stretch itself out about **twenty times** its normal length, and then squeeze into tight spaces.

Butterflies taste with their feet.

An ant can lift **ten times** its own body weight.

When you feel an itch, you scratch it because your brain thinks it might be an insect trying to suck your blood.

The greatest number of **bee stings** ever survived is 2,243. Ouch!

Spiders have **48 knees** – eight legs with six joints on each.

BIGGEST, SMALLEST, FASTEST, TALLEST . . .

Biggest overall – the blue whale is the largest living mammal at up to 34 metres long – that's the length of four double-decker buses – and 150 tonnes – that's more than the weight of 21 elephants.

Biggest land animal – the African bush elephant, weighing nearly seven tonnes.

Tallest land animal – the giraffe, which can be over six metres tall – as tall as your house.

Tallest known human was 2.73 metres tall. If you sit on your dad's shoulders you'll get some idea how big that is.

Smallest mammal – pygmy shrews, weighing less than six grams, the same as a 50p piece.

Smallest bird – the hummingbird weighs 28 grams – even less than a small bag of crisps.

Smallest known human was 56cm small – just up to the third step of a staircase, or the length of a junior tennis racquet.

Fattest animals – ringed seal pups. Half of their body is fat!

Fattest known human was 636 kilograms – that's approximately 18 tubby two-week-old seal pups!

Fastest animal – the cheetah, running at speeds of up to 100 kilometres per hour. Ask your mum or dad to tell you when they're driving at around 60 miles an hour – that's how fast the cheetah can run!

Fastest human ran at 37.3 kilometres per hour. This is around your driving speed in a 20 miles per hour zone — feels slow in the car, but it's fast on foot.

Fastest swimmer — the dolphin — at 56 kilometres per hour — that's nearly 19 lengths in a minute.

That's almost as fast as I can swim. Just ask Soggy Sid if you don't believe me.

Fastest bird — the peregrine falcon, which dives on a victim at 290 kilometres per hour, that's as fast as a high-speed train.

Slowest animal — the sloth, which moves at only two kilometres per hour — that's like you walking really slowly.

Highest jumper – kangaroos can jump over three metres high. They can jump over an elephant!

Highest human jump is 2.45 metres high, only a bit lower than the record-breaking kangaroo.

Deepest diver – the Antarctic penguin, diving to depths of 400 metres, almost the length of three and a half football pitches.

Brainiest mammal – human beings.

Brainiest bird – the hummingbird has the largest brain, which is nearly half of its total body weight.

Longest life – Asian elephants live nearly as long as humans, with the oldest one ever living to 78.

Longest human life – 122 years and 164 days.

Largest ears – the African elephant at
2 × 1.5 metres, about the size of a sheet
for a double bed.

GROWING
PAINS

Between the ages of 6 and 12, you might feel pain in your legs during the night. Don't worry, it just means you're growing taller very fast!

When you're a teenager, you'll really spurt up in height, sometimes growing up to **9cm a year**.

Your brain stops growing when you are 15 years old.

But I think Peter's stopped growing ages ago.

Babies have **really big heads**! About a quarter of a baby's height is its head, but grown-ups' heads are only an eighth of their height.

Ask your mum what time you were born. More babies are born between three and four o'clock in the morning than at any other hour.

Your **nose** and **ears** continue growing throughout your entire life!

Five hundred years ago, not many people lived past the age of 50…

… and not many men grew to more than 1.55 metres tall either, the same height as an average 12-year-old boy today.

Your eyes stay the same size throughout your life, which is why babies have such big eyes.

CAN YOU
DO
THIS . . . ?

 Can you roll up your tongue? If you can, you're not alone – 85% of the population can do it too.

Can you sneeze with your eyes open? It's impossible!

Try eating a **sugary doughnut** without licking your lips. It's difficult because your body's natural instinct is to clean up the mess.

Can you eat more than three cream crackers in a row? You won't be able to because your mouth can't produce enough **saliva** to cope with them.

It's impossible to lick your own elbow –
unless you're very **double-jointed**.
(I bet you just tried it, didn't you?)

Can you pat your head
with one hand and
rub your tummy
at the same time?
Go on – try it!

Sit down, lift your right foot off the floor and make circles with it in a clockwise direction. At the same time, try drawing a number 6. Can you do it?

Can you stand on one leg, arms at your sides, with your eyes closed? You'll be **wobbly** because your balance is affected by your eyesight.

Are you ticklish? If you're happy, being tickled makes you laugh. But if you're feeling worried or sad, you might get upset if someone tickles you.

Have you ever had **pins and needles**? You can get this if you sit in a funny position and squash a nerve.

Try bending your wrist as far as it will go, then clench your fist and see what happens. One of your muscles is overpowering the other.

Rotate the fingers of both your hands in a clockwise direction. Go faster and faster and soon you'll find that your fingers are going in opposite directions.

When you're with a friend, do a big yawn. Your friend will yawn too, because **yawning is infectious**!

Can you juggle with three balls? If you can, that's brilliant but you'll have to beat 12 balls to win the world record.

How long can you stand on one foot?
The world record is 76 hours and 40 minutes!

Do you ever get hiccups? The longest anyone has had hiccups is 69 years!

How do you feel when you've had the giggles? You should feel better, because laughter relaxes your body and is very good for you.

Can you touch your nose or chin with your tongue? Not many people can!

Can you raise one eyebrow, or twitch your nose, or wiggle your ears? If you can, you're very good at controlling your muscles.

Can you say this **tongue twister** fast five times:

If a black bug bleeds black blood,
what colour blood does a blue bug bleed?

Tricky? That's because it's difficult for your brain and tongue to work together.

Bye!

HORRID HENRY BOOKS

Horrid Henry
Horrid Henry and the Secret Club
Horrid Henry Tricks the Tooth Fairy
Horrid Henry's Nits
Horrid Henry Gets Rich Quick
Horrid Henry's Haunted House
Horrid Henry and the Mummy's Curse
Horrid Henry's Revenge
Horrid Henry and the Bogey Babysitter
Horrid Henry's Stinkbomb
Horrid Henry's Underpants
Horrid Henry Meets the Queen
Horrid Henry and the Mega-Mean Time Machine
Horrid Henry and the Football Fiend
Horrid Henry's Christmas Cracker
Horrid Henry and the Abominable Snowman
Horrid Henry Robs the Bank
Horrid Henry Wakes the Dead
Horrid Henry Rocks

Early Readers
Don't Be Horrid, Henry!
Horrid Henry's Birthday Party
Horrid Henry's Holiday
Horrid Henry's Underpants
Horrid Henry Gets Rich Quick
Horrid Henry and the Football Fiend
Horrid Henry's Nits
Horrid Henry and Moody Margaret
Horrid Henry's Thank You Letter

Colour Books

Horrid Henry's Big Bad Book
Horrid Henry's Wicked Ways
Horrid Henry's Evil Enemies
Horrid Henry Rules the World
Horrid Henry's House of Horrors
Horrid Henry's Dreadful Deeds
Horrid Henry Shows Who's Boss

Joke Books

Horrid Henry's Joke Book
Horrid Henry's Jolly Joke Book
Horrid Henry's Might Joke Book
Horrid Henry versus Moody Margaret
Horrid Henry's Hilariously Horrid Joke Book

Activity Books

Horrid Henry's Brainbusters
Horrid Henry's Headscratchers
Horrid Henry's Mindbenders
Horrid Henry's Colouring Book
Horrid Henry's Puzzle Book
Horrid Henry's Sticker Book
Horrid Henry's Classroom Chaos
Horrid Henry's Holiday Havoc
Horrid Henry Runs Riot
Horrid Henry's Annual 2011

Visit Horrid Henry's website at
www.horridhenry.co.uk
for competitions, games, downloads and a monthly newsletter.